I0152989

When I stand before God at the end of my life, I would hope that I would not have a single bit of talent left and could say, I used everything you gave me.

Erma Bombeck

How to Accomplish Almost Anything with

POSITIVE ACCOUNTABILITY

The First Step to Success

How to Accomplish Almost Anything with

POSITIVE ACCOUNTABILITY
The First Step to Success

Royce White

READnLEAD PUBLISHING

Copyright © 2014 by Royce W. White

All rights reserved. In accordance with the U.S. Copyright Act of 1976, the scanning, uploading, and electronic sharing of any part of this book without the permission of the publisher constitute unlawful piracy and theft of the author's intellectual property. If you would like to use material from the book (other than for review purposes), prior written permission must be obtained by contacting the publisher by email at

permissions@readnleadpublishing.com.

Thank you for your support of the author's rights.

ReadnLead Publishing
PO Box 861587
Vint Hill Farms, VA 20187
www.readnleadpublishing.com
www.twitter.com/readnleadpub

First e-book edition: November 2014
First Audio Book edition: December 2014
The ReadnLead name and logo are trademarks of ReadnLead Publishing.

The publisher is not responsible for websites (or their content) that are not owned by the publisher.

ISBN-13: 978-0-9862457-0-1
ISBN-10: 0-9862-4570-4

Cover Design: Design Eye, 2014 © Royce White
Cover Photo: 2009 © Vernon Wiley Photography

Dedication

To my family—

To my five children and my bride of 36 years (as of 2014).
Thank you for helping me grow and learn and take life head-on.
I love you all and appreciate your hearts for the
difference you make in the world.

Table of Contents

Acknowledgments

Beloved Poppa John Maxwell—for saying yes to the call beyond motivational speaking to leadership training and pouring into me so much through your mentorship, books, speaking, and more... I've learned much because of your faithfulness. *My name is Royce, and I'm your friend!* I'm so thankful for your heart and your labor of love. Blessings!

Christian Simpson—for your passion and expertise at the *Art, Science, and Practice of Professional Coaching.* You are truly the guru of coaching, and a humble one at that. I appreciate you very much. Thanks for your patience with all my questions, thoughts, comments, ad nauseum over the years. You're the bomb!

JMT Mentors—Scott, Ed, Roddy, Melissa, Paul... Thanks for pouring into us all. We are better because you give. Yes, it's your business to do this and you get paid to do it, but thanks for going beyond the call and doing it with fearless abandon and delight. You make it easy and fun to learn!

Jody—thanks for being the most beautiful and wonderful woman in the world-oh, and for your awesome *ain't-nobody-better* editing skills. You make me sound better than I am! I'm glad I ~~choose~~ chose wisely! I love you!

Julie Randall—thanks for pushing me to make this book happen. Your simple challenge to get it done pushed me off of the fence and positively held me accountable! I'm still going to finish before you! Don't Drive Angry!

Dad—thanks for all the training you did give me and for teaching me that *the toughest part of getting started IS getting started!* You really did teach me all *you* know! I love you...

Dana Morgan Barnes (oh skinny one) & Bart Breen—unbeknownst to either of you, your winning battles to lose the weight and make your lives better has inspired and encouraged me all along my journey writing this book. Thank you!

My *beloved* family and friends on the *John Maxwell Team.* Your insight, passion for leadership, love, kindness, and desire to make an impact for good on the entire world inspires me to write, speak, and teach. May you have continued success throughout eternity. I love you all! Many blessings...

And finally, to the King of Glory... because You Are. What do I have that You didn't give and what do I know that You didn't tell...

Introduction

"Clean up your room or…"
"Get the report in by COB today or…"
"Pay what you owe or…"

Negative accountability—do this or else. It's a major part of life. It's what drives us in almost everything from a necessity perspective... yet the word makes our skin crawl, leaves a bad taste in our mouths, and is compared to having a root canal. In fact, a recent (2014) Zogby poll shows that a majority of those surveyed feel that accountability is something negative that happens to them—usually when things go wrong—rather than something they utilize to ensure success.[1] But what if we could shift perspective and achieve accountability from a positive perspective?

In almost everything, we are accountable to an outside force. It's a *negative* influence for good. We drive the speed limit for fear of getting a ticket. We pay our taxes on time because we fear paying the penalty or the government hauling us away. We keep our weight down and in shape when we aren't in a relationship for fear of not attracting a mate. We at least put on the appearance of work at our job for fear of being fired. The list goes on and on and on… FILL IN THE BLANKS, write your own list. Even so, for the most part we just do enough to get by. We push the speed limit by 5-10 mph because that's the most we can push it and not get stopped. We pay our taxes on time, though 41% of us pay within the last 30 days before they're due—27% in the last 15 days.[2] We keep our weight down when pursuing the catch, but we put on the "freshman 15" after we're caught.

Think of your life and all the things you do because something or someone is holding you accountable. The whole legal system is set up to keep people accountable to social norms. We are inundated with accountability. Without it, we would quickly be led by our selfish nature and lowest level—our "Lord of the Flies," if you will.[3] Without the alarm clock, we will sleep in. Without the "Oil Alert" on our car, we would burn up the engine. Without "Siri" (iPhone) reminding us of this or that meeting, we would be late. If no one enforced our being at work or school, we would not go on days we didn't feel like going. Without speed limit enforcement, every road would be the Autobahn. (A.D.D. Moment: I love the signs on the Virginia highways that say "Speed *Enforced* by Aircraft." Enforced? Does that mean they are going to shoot at us to *enforce* the speed limit?)

At this point, somewhere between 15-24% of you are saying to yourselves, "this is bunk—I do this because it's what needs to be done." True. But you are the ~20% of the population that *are* self-starters.[4] The rest of us have to have a great reason to get started! Even so, I know plenty of self-starters that have this problem from time to time. It just depends upon what we're dealing with at that time.

One of my mentors, John Maxwell, tells the story of a time when he was speaking to a group, and a young college student came running up to him during a break; and, waving his index finger with intensity, he said to John, "I am rushed for time. Tell me—what is the one thing in leadership I need to know?" Answering the young man with equal intensity and the waving of his index finger, John said, "The one thing you need to know about leadership, is that there is more than one thing to know about leadership!" John's *21 Irrefutable Laws of Leadership*,

15 Invaluable Laws of (personal) *Growth*, and *The 17 Indisputable Laws of Teamwork* prove that point. As a matter of fact, I have no need to write anything on leadership because John covered the general subject so well (as well as Brian Tracy, Zig Ziglar, Les Brown, and a host of others).

Indeed, to become a good-to-great leader, a study of John's books will get you well on your way, and eventually to a level 5 leader—IF… you learn ***AND*** apply (did I emphasize the ***AND*** enough??). But as I worked with entrepreneurs, others on the John Maxwell Team, and people in general, most of them—80% of them—suffered from what my dad used to define as "the toughest part about getting started, is getting started."[5]

Everybody is "going to write that book." (81% of the population say they *have a book in them*.[6]) But only .2% do it (that's *point* 2!), and all of the 81% are well meaning. Everybody is going to start *that* company, but only 13% of them do.[7] 59% say we are overweight. 54% say we are going to lose weight. 25% say we are serious. The average weight we want to lose? 18 pounds. Only about 15% of us do and then most (about 85%) of us put the weight back on. What is going on in our hearts *and* minds that causes us *not* to begin and then, if we do, to vacillate so wildly? How can we accomplish that which constantly eludes us?

Accountability. Think about it. What if we took the principle that is so pervasive and invasive in our lives—accountability for legal/necessary things—and applied those principles and feelings to our CHOICES as well—things that we WANT to accomplish. I love and teach John Maxwell's laws on leadership and personal growth. The hard part for most of my mentees / coaching clients / others, is indeed getting started—and once started, staying on target. Mere planning won't ensure that they take their goal past the planning stage. Execution of those plans is essential. In *my* survey and study, only 2% of the population FULLY plans each day and only another 2% follow the specific *action items* they set up in that plan daily. We plan in order to feel good about the day because we know we should, but we don't achieve all that we can. Brian Tracy's book *Eat That Frog*[8] is a great book to help us understand procrastination and develop a strategy to move ahead. But we need more than a strategy—we need accomplishment—we need the win.

It's like knowledge. You've heard it said that "knowledge is power" or knowledge is the key to success. *Not true.* If it were true we would all be rich. *APPLIED* knowledge is power. Yes we need to know *how to* accomplish. But even more, we need accomplishment to *happen*—and for that, we need… accountability. We won't do it without it… guaranteed… unless we're in that 20% of self starters. Even so...

This book will show you how to best define *your* success and move past the things you are not doing to get to the success you desire. Not just in business and leadership, but personally. As a matter of fact, it needs to happen in the personal realm first for it to be applied to the business realm.

I have deliberately kept this book short so we can get through it quickly without getting sidetracked. Besides, this isn't rocket science needing significant math—it's a pragmatic book of methodologies and procedures. This is not a get-rich-quick book, although practicing Positive Accountability as a life methodology will help you make an order of magnitude[9] more than living in constant procrastination and non-accomplishment. It is not a book about time management, though some aspects of time management are discussed. It is a book for using accountability in a *positive*, tenacious way to accomplish your goals and desires—to get you where you want to go!

This book is not about procrastination, although that is a part of not self-finishing and I do have solutions throughout the book, and it's not about 12 things you must do to succeed—it is about the *one* thing that if put into place *first*, will naturally and perpetually move you through to a greater success. Will you still need knowledge? Yep. Will you still need 21 laws of this and that? Absolutely. So why do I say it's the FIRST step to success? Because the key to getting started, the push to learn and do the homework necessary, and the glue keeping you on target, is found in *Positive Accountability*—and I'm going to show you how to embrace it and use it to the fullest for your success.

Live long and prosper; be accountable and succeed!

Royce White
Warrenton, VA
November 2014

IMPORTANT! READ THIS...

I've noticed over the years that in most really good non-fiction books I've read, there is a lot more material in the book than just the "how to do" something. There is a lot of supporting material deeper points to convince me of an idea. I catch myself thinking, "I just want to know how to do it! Just give me the specifics—you don't need to convince me!" Of course, in many cases, I DO need convincing; though in many I do not. Why mention this?

There are points in this book I need to get across as part of the whole process of *Positive Accountability*. I could just give you the straight-up list of what to do. But without the "why," some of it doesn't make sense. Or it may make sense, but if you knew the purpose, it would make it a whole lot easier to get behind the concept and do it. Hence, don't despair with the lead-in material to the actual action items. This is a simple book and won't take you more than two hours to read anyway. Knowing how you define success (Chapter 2) and knowing balance (Chapter 4) are crucial elements to get extreme results.

I also need to say that you must WANT to be successful. If you have limiting beliefs or fears, or are unsure of what you need to do, you need to get a good coach first. On my website, there is a list of coaches that get great results *with* their current clients and I highly recommend them (also in the Appendix). Check out roycewhite.com and look for the menu item called *Coaches*.

Also—the "he/she" thing—you know— "... he or she, him or her..." I hate that. It wastes a lot of my time writing it and your time reading it. I use one or the other gender throughout the text to mean "both guys and girls!" (I say "he said" or "she did" etc.). If you see one there, please assume the other as well. Either one means "he or she"—fill in the other in your mind please. Thank you!

Finally, I use a lot of *italics* in this book. When you read them, *hugely emphasize* the word—it will help you get my point better. Or go buy the audio version of this book (which is read by me)—you'll get my emphasis *perfectly*...

Now, on to Positive Accountability!

"MOTIVATION
gets you started.
HABIT
keeps you going."

Jim Rohn

— 1 —

Defining Positive Accountability

**"Every excuse I ever heard made perfect
sense to the person who made it."**
— Dr. Daniel T. Drubin —

It was a typical cloudy day in London. It was early May. I was on my
semi-annual tour of my company's European Reps. As the Marketing
VP, I visited them all twice a year to train, help, encourage, motivate,
etc. I had some time before my afternoon meeting with my UK Rep,
so I was at Piccadilly Circus eating lunch at a fast-food restaurant on
my way to a music store to see what wondrous old saxophones they
might have. I am a jazz saxophonist and I am always looking for the
perfect find—a very old Selmer Mark 6 Cigar Cutter alto sax for little-
to-no money.

I finished my lunch and stepped onto the sidewalk with my large
chocolate shake in my hand. I generally knew the direction, so I head-
ed off toward the store. As I reached the curb, I looked left and stepped
into the street. WHAM! I was stopped cold in my tracks, leaning into
the street as a London Cab whooshed by merely an inch from my
nose. I could see my reflection in the Cabby's window...

Suddenly, I was jerked back to the sidewalk. I looked down at the pressure on my chest—it was a strong arm belonging to a tall British fellow next to me. He looked very much like the 1972 version of the actor Stephen Boyd, only taller and skinnier. The obvious interview ensued... "You're not from around here" he said with a heavy Yorkshiremen accent—more of a statement than a question.

"What gave you that idea?" I returned, trying to gain my composure as my subconscious slowly stopped flashing my life before my eyes...

With profundity he quipped, "Well, you look to the left instead of the right when crossing, and you're carrying your drink around with you—we don't do that here." Fair enough.

We talked for a while and I bought him some lunch for saving my life. It was the least I could do. Then he bid me farewell, reminded me to look right instead of left, and wished me a good life. Moments earlier, I was a feather away from serious injury or even death. I really can still see my reflection in the cab if I think about it. Had he not been around, my life would be very different today. I don't know if he was an angel or a homeless guy—but I am very thankful he was there. Very. Uber. Totally. Yep.

Sometimes we need a little help to get through the day. It can be as drastic as life-saving, or as simple as a helping hand, an encouragement—a reminder. Most of us can achieve the simple things in life by ourselves. But there are times when we need some *help* to accomplish- to succeed. *That* day, I needed some serious help and, thankfully, I received it.

This book is about how to get the help you need to succeed—and *actually* use it to succeed. It's also about personal growth, and *learning* to succeed on your own. The methodology is not difficult, but don't let that tempt you to dismiss it. If you follow it, you have better than 90% chance of accomplishing what you start.

I love the story in antiquity of Naaman, the commander of the army of the king of Aram, who was a valiant soldier and had the love of his master. He was wealthy and well known. He only had one problem... he had an incurable disease—leprosy. There was a young girl captured from his enemy that was serving his wife, and she told Naaman about a prophet that could cure him of his leprosy. So, he went to the prophet, and the prophet told him to wash in the Jordan River seven times and his flesh would be restored and his leprosy would be gone. Naaman was enraged and said, "I thought that the prophet would surely come out to me and stand and call on the name of his God, wave his hand over the spot, and cure me of my leprosy." Then he huffed off.

Naaman's servants ran after him and said, "My father, if the prophet had told you to do some great thing, would you not have done it? How much more, then, when he tells you, 'Wash and be cleansed'!" So Naaman went down and dipped himself in the river seven times, as the prophet had told him, and his flesh was restored and became clean like that of a young boy.[10]

The point of the story is that what the prophet asked Naaman to do was *not* hard—in fact, it was quite easy. The problem was that he was too proud to do it. Like the prophet's instructions, what I am going to share with you is *not* hard to do—it is fairly easy. You may be ready to climb Mount Everest, swim the English Channel, or do some other great feat to succeed—but it's not necessary in order to *get started*. "It is always wise to look ahead, but difficult to look further than you can see"—Winston Churchill. The real work is getting and staying on target. And like the story of Naaman, the outcome for doing this simple thing can have an amazing effect on your life, making you a master of accomplishment. Not only will it get you started, it will take you to the finish line.

Accountability. It's a trending buzzword (at least when this book was written). There are quite a few good books out there recently on how to hold your team, your coworkers, yourself, and others accountable. It's all about *how* we deal with it—the *what* is pretty simple (you didn't do what you said you would!). I see many courses and consulting companies teaching on how to deal with accountability—which is good.

It's a very hard subject because we don't like to be held accountable for our actions or lack thereof. These are all *after* the fact, or problem accountabilities—meaning an expectation wasn't met, you didn't do what you said you would, etc. This *is* accountability, but it's what I call *negative* accountability—we have to deal with a problem *after* the problem happened. Some things do require a negative accountability, but what I want to teach is a way to accomplish beforehand—in a positive way—so we hopefully won't ever get to needing the negative accountability.

Wouldn't it be awesome to never have to be held accountable for what you didn't accomplish because you accomplished it??

Positive Accountability is also accountability, still one person working with another, but it happens *before*. That's right—before. It's not dealing with something because something got messed up, it's dealing with it from the idea stage to give it *power* to be accomplished. It's like good management. You do it because you *planned* to do it, *purposed* to do it, and *proceeded* to do it!

Snake oil. I am not making promises that (say this with a used car salesman's radio voice...) "If you follow this exactly as I have laid it out, you will become a HUGE success!!" Though I believe you will. No snake oil here.[11] But I *am* saying that this methodology does work for a lot of people—most people—people like you and me—and like a positive attitude will always help you get more done than a negative attitude will, you have a much better chance of accomplishing if you work with *Positive Accountability*.

I don't know about you, but I want all my cylinders firing and the best chance at success I can muster. I know for me and *my* coach (yes, I have a coach), as well as for *my* coaching clients, when we hold one another accountable, we succeed much more quickly than without accountability. It really is a serious part of the coaching trade and a serious part of accomplishing. If we can do it ourselves, all the better—that's our ultimate goal—to learn to accomplish on our own. But most of us are *not* self-starters and need a little help until we learn to become self-starters. Positive Accountability *is* that help.

Leadership expert John Maxwell, in his book *The 15 Invaluable Laws of Growth*,[12] one of my top recommended reads (go get it now, and I do mean now—you'll thank me one day), in Chapter 1, "The

Law of Intentionality," talks about *growth gaps*. We think because we *naturally* grew when we were younger, we should *naturally* grow now. Not so. You must be *intentional* about your growth—it won't just happen. So our ultimate goal is to be an *intentional self-starter and an intentional self-finisher*. But until we get there, and even for a while after, and even from time-to-time when things are very difficult, Positive Accountability will allow us to start succeeding *today* and anytime.

Why I Wrote This Book

It's hard to get started—and as you will learn, most of us are *not* self-starters. I certainly wasn't the best self-starter. Fortunately for me, there have been a couple of people in my life that have gone out of their way to help me. I am very grateful to them. I want to give back and I love adding value to people. I *want* to see you succeed!

I also love getting to the cause. Logic dictates it for me. I hate just knowing the symptoms—whether it's in the doctor's office, the company's office, or the home office. I want to know the cause, the core, the root, the bottom line, the reason. I guess it's the marketing guy in me. I love the truth, even when it hurts. Living a lie only hurts more later on in all spheres of life. I haven't always loved the truth. I fail at it from time to time, but I do love what is true.

Through coaching, being a CEO, working with people and companies for 37 years, I've seen that we all have different abilities—similar desires, but different abilities and goals. Getting to accomplishment is hard for many people, possibly most people. I wanted to get at the root of why some people accomplish and others don't—or why some accomplish faster than others. I also discovered that self-help *alone* doesn't always work—not with all of the 80% of *non*-self-starters. As a matter of fact, it doesn't *seem* to work most of the time. Or rather, only on a small segment of the 80%. Granted, with the low number of people that read, that number won't change much over time. If it did, we would only need one self-help book and we would all change and all be rich and famous. Not that it doesn't need to be sought after and applied—it does. But again, the creatures of habit that we are make it difficult to achieve success much of the time—without a little help from our friends...

I have been looking for the answer to why we don't change—and why it takes so long for those that do. Most importantly, I've been looking for a solution for the problem—if only a temporary solution— or a *bridge* solution—and I believe I found it. That's what Positive Accountability is all about. Until we learn to be awesome self-starters, Positive Accountability will get us going and get us accomplishing. Like my dad, the incredible engineer, always asks, "What are you trying to optimize?" I want to optimize *accomplishment* for everybody that reads this book. I want to help everybody get ahead. I want to provide a solution for those that find it hard to get started *and* get finished. I hope this helps you as much as it has helped me.

Reflection and Journaling

Face it. We don't reflect much on what we do. We're not thinkers as much as doers. We like to think we are, but we are more simple-action oriented than thought oriented. We "Do," we eat, we sleep, we get up and Do again. We don't always do what we're supposed to do, or the right thing, but we are constantly—busy (busyness does not equate to accomplishment). Based upon my specific research (asking people "do you keep a personal reflection journal at least once a week, not including a blog?"), the number of people that intentionally journal their thoughts or their day is miniscule... under a percent (how many people do you know who journal daily or at all?).

Without reflection, we cannot hold ourselves accountable. Unless we get in real trouble or *intentionally* want to repeat a situation, we don't think about what happened in our day and how we can *grow* from it. Very few of us have a plan for personal growth—we just *Do Life.* Just ask all your friends if they have a specific plan for *personal growth*- you'll be astonished at the seriously undefined answers. First, they will ask you to explain what you mean. Then, they will take a while to answer. Then, you'll notice that they will tell of their current or past accomplishments. Then, after you bring them back on target, they will say, "I guess not."

According to a study on *StatisticsBrain*, only about 58% of people read after college.[13] That means that 42 percent of us don't intentionally study/read to improve ourselves. (My guess is it's probably bigger than half who *don't* because it's tough to confess you don't read.) We figure we've done that enough already. No need to be accountable to ourselves (or anyone else). No need to grow. You read, you lead... or not.

Total percentage of U.S. families who did *not* buy a book this year? 80%.[13] Further, the total percentage of books started that aren't read to completion is 57%. If you take the 58% of the people that *do* read (from last paragraph) and multiply it by 43% (the percentage of those that *do* finish the book they start), you get a whopping 25% of us who finish a book. That's downright scary to me. What percentage of those are fiction books?? Not that entertainment is bad—it's not—but if we're not working to continually grow, we stay right where we are—or worse—regress. We're not growing or moving toward accomplishment.

As well, we don't like to be told what to do—even though we might be only one step away from stupid. It's deeply ingrained in us. Maybe it's the *rugged individualism* we've encountered all our lives. Call it pride, call it stupidity, we don't like to be told what to do (see Naaman's story above and countless stories in your own life as well as others you know). Do you know the difference between dumb and stupid? Dumb is not knowing any better. Stupid is knowing better but doing it anyway.

So, in a way, we don't like to be held accountable. Nobody I know would ever confess that, but we sure do hate to be nagged by anyone. So we don't like accountability from ourselves *or* from others either.

It goes something like this—

MOM: "Royce, is your homework done? No dinner tonight until you've done your homework."

DAD: "Royce, is the lawn mowed? No dinner for a week if it's not done by bedtime."

SIS: "Hey Bozo—are you going to return my book? No dinner for the rest of your life, which will be very short unless you get it back by tomorrow morning."

DOG: "Where's my dinner?"

ME: "WUFF!"

Life really is too short to have people nagging at you 24/7. Even the telesales people whine and nag at us (Telesales Person: "Yes, I know you have 37 reasons why you won't buy, but I have 38 objections to your 37 reasons!!").

Most of us don't plan well either—and we execute the action items taken from our planning more badly, and are constantly forgetting and being chided in one way or another. Not because we're bad people, but typically because we haven't learned to be *intentional* or learned the secret to accomplishing. Those above you scold—those under you complain. We aren't listening...

Positive Accountability is not...

So let's start with what *Positive Accountability* is NOT. It's not a personal or business scolding or a situation where you must do or die- or have something negative happen as a result. Those things may happen anyway, but *we* are not going to attack it from a negative perspective *after* the fact—logically that won't work *before* the fact, and that rarely works after we've failed as well (negative input). We're going to attack it positively—*before* we attempt it.

The problem of not accomplishing can be many fold—too much to do, don't know how to plan and/or execute, too many *urgent* and not enough *important* things on your plate, lazy, whatever, fill in the blank. That's not the concern of *this* book. Hopefully, I can address those issues in later books. The problem of not getting things done is real for a variety of reasons. This methodology will put into place a type of accountability that will help you succeed at almost anything.

A note to the twenty percenters (20%)... you've already got what it takes to get started. Whether you were born with that self-starting personality, learned it from your parents or events in life, embraced it later in life because you learned it's the only way to get accomplishing—or whatever reason, don't beat up on the 80% who struggle with getting started. There's a big desire to say "JUST DO IT!!"—but that only works for a small portion of us. Again, if it worked all the time for everybody, we wouldn't have the 80%. It has to be learned. We have to *see* accomplishment in our own lives first—small wins—learn the process, learn to be a self-finisher. Then saying *just do it* will begin to work. We're not dumb (nor stupid), we process differently—just as introverts and extroverts process differently, yet both are needed.

Positive Accountability is...

So what does Positive Accountability (PA) mean? What are we talking about? How will it help you?

What if you made a *decision* to do something—a choice. Let's start with something everybody understands—losing weight. The negatives are fairly obvious. If I eat this I will gain weight—a moment on the lips, a lifetime on the hips. If I don't exercise, I will be more tired and not able to do as much—no pain, no gain. I'm overweight and I don't look good. If I don't lose weight, nobody will like me, etc., etc... So we set up a program and away we go. January 2nd the gyms are full... until about January 21. Then they're back to normal—lots of open parking spaces. We gave up. Lost 4 pounds—all water weight. I'm thirsty...

A 2010 study published in the *Journal of the American Medical Association (JAMA)* found that 92% of the participants in a Jenny Craig weight loss program stuck with it for two years.[14] 92%! For two years! That's amazing! That's huge! That's gigantinormous! Now I know why they have so much money to run all those TV ads. So why do Jenny Craig, Nutrisystem, and related companies have a great success rate for helping you lose weight? Because *they* are your personal trainer, your personal coach. Same for debt reduction companies—the honest ones that is. There is someone holding your hand—some, most, or all of the way to accomplishment, and it makes it much easier—or maybe just more attainable... same for Positive Accountability.

I mentioned in the "Introduction" something my dad used to always say—"the hardest part of getting started, is getting started." It is enormously hard and takes a lot of inertia to go from no motion *to* motion. Newton's first law of motion says, "An object at rest stays at rest and an object in motion stays in motion with the same speed and in the same direction unless acted upon by an unbalanced force." Positive Accountability Translation: unless something pushes you, you won't do it, and if you do it, not in a timely manner, and if in a timely manner, you won't finish it, and if you... you get the idea.

So we have this theory of something not happening unless a force makes it happen. If the force is not in you, then it has to come from somewhere else. Interestingly enough, the ability *is* in you, you just haven't been trained to bring it out. Executive/Life/Confidence Coaching can help you discover it and bring it out.

Coaching

I am a firm believer in coaching because I see it work time and time again in my own life, my own coaching practice, as well as in many other peers' coaching practices. Actually, let me change that from "*a firm believer*"—that makes it sound like it is based upon faith alone—to "*has a proven track record*"—because I see the ACTUAL results from coaching every day (thank you Christian Simpson[15]). People stuck with all kinds of situations are coached to a greater success over a much shorter period of time than if left to fend for themselves.

So why not get coaching instead of learning and utilizing Positive Accountability? Good question! Great question! A coaching question! Coaching is used to help people dig deep to find the answers that are inside and put those truths to work for them in solving problems, getting beyond limiting beliefs, meeting high-level goals, dealing with a myriad of problems and "stuckness,"etc. As well, it costs a lot more than utilizing Positive Accountability.

Coaches are trained, qualified, and certified. Coaching has its place and its time. Positive Accountability does not build a relationship (rapport) intentionally, does not bring out the depths of the heart and mind and apply it to solving life's needs, nor does it find out many options and a way forward. It needs little understanding and training and anyone can do it. Positive Accountability simply deals with a KNOWN task and helps you get on AND stay on target to get it done—just like Jenny Craig.

Building Habits—The 21 Day Myth

Why does this work? It's all in the Brain. Once we *build* a habit, we can continue that habit until success—and the more we continue, the better the chance of success. But during the building of the habit, we gyrate all over the place, starting and stopping, making excuses, etc.

There is a general myth about how long it takes to build a habit. Many quote 21 days like it is a known fact.[16] Dr. Maxwell Maltz, who is the father of a lot of today's Leadership principles and author of the 1970s book *Psycho-Cybernetics*, was quoted as saying that it takes 21 days to build a habit. This is a misrepresentation of his study on self-esteem habit building. It appears that the concept grew simply because people wanted it to be true—which happens often in society. (Remember the concept of Lemmings? They follow each other off a cliff? It's a farce. Untrue. Perpetuated by Disney.[17] Not everything is as it appears.

What is the reality of building a habit? Tom Bartow, who started advanced training for Edward Jones and is a highly sought after business coach, and Dr. Jason Selk, developed the following model of what habit formation *really* looks like:

The 3 Phases of Habit Formation:[18]

Phase 1: THE HONEYMOON

This phase of habit formation is characterized by the feeling of "this is easy." As all married people will tell you, at some point even the greatest honeymoon must end. The honeymoon phase is usually the result of something inspiring. For example, a person attends a highly motivational conference, and for the first few days after the conference the individual is making positive changes in his or her life.

Phase 2: THE FIGHT THRU

Inspiration fades and reality sets in. A person finds himself struggling with the positive habit completion and old habits seem to be right around the corner. The key to moving to the third phase of habit formation is to win 2 or 3 "fight thru's." This is critical. To win the fight thru, use the following techniques:

RECOGNIZE: Recognition is essential for winning the fight thru. When you have entered the fight through, simply say to yourself, "I have entered the fight thru, and I need to win a few to move past this." Winning each fight thru will make it easier to win the next. Conversely, when you choose to lose a fight thru, you make it easier to lose the next one.

ASK 2 QUESTIONS: "How will I feel if I do this?" and "How will I feel if I don't do this?" Bring EMOTION into the equation. Let yourself feel the positive in winning the fight thru and the negative in losing.

LIFE PROJECTION: If the above 2 techniques haven't moved you to action, then imagine in great detail how your life will be in 5 years if you do not begin making changes. Be totally honest with yourself, and allow yourself to feel what life will be like if the changes are not made.

Phase 3: SECOND NATURE

Entering second nature is often described by feelings of "getting in the groove." Once in second nature, the following are 3 common interruptions that will send a person back to the fight thru:

THE DISCOURAGEMENT MONSTER: An individual allows negative results discourage him or her into thinking, "This isn't working, and there is nothing I can do."

DISRUPTIONS: An individual experiences significant change to his or her current pattern (e.g., vacations, holidays, illness, weekends).

SEDUCTION OF SUCCESS: An individual begins to focus on positive results and begins to think, "I'm the special one. I have finally figured out how to have great results with not so great process."

First we are excited to get started. Next, we are struggling to complete the habit process daily. Finally, we feel like we're in the groove and winning. Yea, that sums it up nicely. The problem is, most of us cop out in phase two when the going gets tough and never get to phase three—especially the non-self-starters. Nonetheless, I think the process is generally a good one, and adding Positive Accountability to it will only add to one's opportunity for success.

So how do you build a habit if you cannot stay on target? That's the real question. Many things are doomed to failure because we don't have the tenacity to *get* tenacity! DOH! So what should we do?

We don't like to let people down—especially if they are helping us stay on target. Even if they are strangers. Even if they fail you. In general, we don't like to disappoint people—which is what you will do if you don't accomplish the task at hand, thereby helping Positive Accountability gain traction. Abraham Lincoln said, "I'm a success today because I had a friend who believed in me and I didn't have the heart to let him down."

Honest Abe isn't the only one. Most of us hate to let people down. If you are checking in with me to help keep me on target with something I have asked your help with, I feel like I will let you down if I don't accomplish, and, hence, I want to, or I am compelled to do it. On the other hand, if you're constantly reminding me to do something I know needs to be done and I DIDN'T ask your help, I feel like it's nagging and the reaction is not good.

Case and Point

Peer pressure is enormous—at almost any age. Author Malcolm Gladwell, in his book *The Tipping Point*, talks of how peer pressure (societal pressure) has more affect on your outcome than does family upbringing. Wherein I believe it is "both and," not "either or," peer pressure is huge. It can be used for ill or good.

I recall a coworker of mine describing one of the questions on a government security form he had to fill out to get a clearance. He was concerned because one of the questions was written in such a way that he could not answer it honestly—his honest answer was predetermined by the questionnaire as not usable. The questionnaire asked if he had ever taken illegal drugs and what the reason for taking them was. It also said he couldn't cite "peer pressure" as the reason. He laughed and shook his head. Peer pressure was pretty much the *only* reason we did things back in high school.

A final note on habits. My bride is fond of saying that building a healthy diet is a lifelong process—it's a way of life—a permanent attitude and lifestyle change. Possibly why the 12-Steps Program calls alcoholics *recovering* alcoholics—no one ever arrives, you have to be diligent—always—it's a lifelong process. I think the same is true for all addictions—and I think the same is true for building *and* breaking habits. We need to get started, stay on target, and fight the battles as we go—always. I do believe it gets easier to battle as time goes on and as we build muscle/brain memory. So we need to get and stay on target.

What does it take?

So Positive Accountability requires two people—the person desiring to be held accountable, and the person holding another accountable. Moreover, it is working with a horizontal peer—*not* with a boss, spouse, or subordinate. A stranger can also be a powerful ally in PA. New beginnings are great because we are starting fresh with someone and have the opportunity to look our best—no baggage hanging around from our past failures.

We won't share enough with our boss or subordinate and hence, we'll be programmed for failure. Same holds true for our spouse. We can struggle with them on so many levels that the task at hand is doomed to failure. No, it is best accomplished with someone we respect who is horizontal with us in relationship. Or, someone we know nothing about—someone we don't know or someone who is *also* interested in having an accountability partner.

The idea is for this to be a positive experience, not a negative one. We're not doing this because if we don't we will get in trouble, but we are planning this ahead of time to ensure success of the project. Chapter 5, "Laying the Foundation of Positive Accountability," will go into detail about how this works, how to set it up and how to do it.

Coming up...

The next chapter, 2, is about "you" defining success. What? How did that work it's way into this book? Henry Ford said, "If everyone is moving forward *together*, then success takes care of itself." We all need reasons to do things. If they are not compelling enough, we won't do them. As it is, 80% of us are not self starters—no matter how much we want to be—we are not... yet. But we still want to succeed! Positive Accountability is a methodology and procedure of how to succeed— or at least how to get started on your way to success. It is so simple, it allows you to easily get started. And the great thing is you apply it to all the things you want to accomplish. So if you know Positive Accountability, you know how to accomplish almost anything else.

Knowing how you define success helps you decide what to do and how much to put into it. For instance, if you define success as working full-time at $20,000 a year, you can do just about anything and succeed at that. You don't need much, if any, accountability—except to get up to go to work. 1970s-1980s actor and author Woody Allen said "Eighty percent of success is showing up." He was definitely on to something.

On the other hand, if you want to be an artist, doctor, or millionaire by the time you're 30, you've got a lot to plan, a lot to accomplish, and need a lot of accountability to get there. So stating your definition of success will help you decide how much accountability you need. Or, maybe you don't know what to do—you're stuck—then you need to jump right in with coaching instead.

Positive Accountability won't help you define or search out anything, it will just help you stay on target with things that you *already* know or stay on target to learn / do things you want to learn and do and be. For those deeper things, you need to move up to coaching.

I find that some coaching can be better handled simply by having a good accountability partner instead. Nothing new needs to be discovered, the client simply needs someone to help her stay on target. I want to move beyond that in coaching so we can concentrate on the bigger issues that need a coaching relationship in order to succeed. For these simple things, I recommend Positive Accountability—a good accountability partner.

A Final Thought

In Chet Holme's excellent book on sales, *The Ultimate Sales Machine*,[19] his mantra is "You *must* be pig-headed!" in your resolve to accomplish. If I could sum up *his* book, *this* book, *any* book, and *most* situations in life, it would be that tenacity—pigheadedness—is the key to success. Slow and *steady* wins the race. Those that start have an opportunity to finish. Those that *don't* start don't get that opportunity. The problem is, much of the time we don't know *how* to start; and, once we do, a large percentage of us—80% of us, the majority of us, most of us, a big bunch of us—don't know how to stay on target. We lack the tenacity—the stick-to-itiveness—to accomplish.

So we need to take this in steps. Would it be best if we could just go from not being good self-starters to being great self-starters? Sure. Definitely. Totally. Abso. But that's not going to happen—not for most of us. Theologian R.C. Sproul puts it best; and, although he's talking about a relationship with God, I think it applies to us all the time in everything. *We will always do what we want most at the moment.* Logical. Makes sense. But we argue that it's not true because we pay our taxes when we don't want to. That sounds good until you add the consequence to the argument: Would you rather pay your taxes and live at peace or not pay your taxes and go to jail? It has to be in context. Because you *do* have a choice. You can choose *not* to pay your taxes—but, you will suffer the consequences. You may choose to suffer those consequences, so your choice to not pay your taxes was what you wanted. See what I mean?

The problem is, most of us have a problem saying no to the good so we can say yes to the great.

Chocolate is good—real good—so good, I'm going to get a piece.... but eating a bunch won't help you get to the slimmer you, the better you. The *great* you (sigh.... guess I won't go get a piece of chocolate). Staying in a good job may be satisfactory but not allow you to get to the great job. Staying in your comfort zone definitely won't allow you to get to those things that stretch you to help you get to the great things of life. Not taking risk may sound good. But taking no risk doesn't allow you to get to the great. No pain, no gain is true in many aspects of life.

The first step in accomplishing—for those of us that lack the personal pigheadedness or tenacity to get and stay on target—is NOT to simply become pigheaded. It sounds good, but that's not the way we are wired—at least not most of us. We have to change our wiring. We have to learn as we go—and I want to get you started NOW. I would love nothing more than to tell you to "just go do it." For so many of us though, it sounds good, get's it off *my* plate (I told you "just do it!"), but then it stalls on your plate (how do I *just do it?*). Those that *are* self-starters (the 20%) and have the tenacity to complete, *can* turn the pigheadedness on and achieve their goals. The rest of us can start *now* by getting a little help while we learn to do it ourselves—and there's nothing wrong with that—in fact, there is everything good about it.

My goal is to get you started *now*, and then have you learn on the way to success how to become a self-starter. Otherwise, we try and try and try and try to turn on a stubborn nature, the tenacity, to no avail—only to fail once again and be in the same place we were. If you can turn it on, do it! And go tackle life. But if you cannot yet, work with someone who will help you get and stay on target—THEN get pig-headed and learn to be that self-starter.

One of our favorite expressions on the John Maxwell Team, is "*Jump and build your wings on the way down.*" That's because most of the people on the Team are more than ready. Been ready. Learned enough. Done enough. Have the expertise. Years, decades, and lifetimes of experience and learning. It's just that the hardest part of getting started, for most people, *is* getting started. But on the Team we have one another to push us. We have built in accountability—and as we jump and move toward success, we help each other push on toward the goal. It's like having a thousand cheerleaders helping you toward your goal. It truly is awesome and amazing.

[Note: this concept, *jump and build your wings on the way down,* is not a reason to be unprepared. You should have your *homework* done and a business model chosen before you jump. Not that you cannot change it as you learn and grow, or as you fail forward—you should. The reason we make this a mantra is because most of our problems are not that we are not ready—it's that there is a fear in us of taking the plunge—the final step to get started. It's another way of saying *do it afraid.*]

This is what accountability is all about. Not beating you up because you failed, but *failing forward* and holding on to one another from the *beginning* to help you succeed from the start. I want to see every person, every family, every company, excel at Positive Accountability. Then, and only then, will people be excited about accountability and embrace it to reach their goal, instead of shying away and hating any encounter with accountability. Why wait until someone fails to hold them accountable? That just doesn't make sense to me. Not that we shouldn't hold people to what they say—we should. But not helping them along the way—especially from the beginning—doesn't make good sense. Isn't that what good management and good leadership are all about—adding value to people so that they can succeed? Remember the words of Zig Ziglar—who I will quote often because he was my first mentor in true motivation and leadership and said what my subconscious remembers best—

"You can have everything in life you want, if you will just help enough other people get what they want."

Which is a good "event memory"—meaning something we learned at an event but don't put into action. Let's add a John Maxwell *teaching moment* on top of that to drive it home—*"To add value to others, one must first value others."* By valuing others and then adding value to them, you will help others gain what they want and need. In turn, you will learn some of the key aspects of leadership and accomplish that which *you* want to accomplish. So helping one another through Positive Accountability *adds value* to the other person—and really doesn't cost you much at all. It's a great investment—for both parties.

Don't despair during this process. Stay on target. Chapter 7 will give you a number of ways to help you stay on target so you can get to success. Apply these principles and teach yourself to do them with tenacity so you will learn to accomplish on your own—which is the second step to real ongoing achievement and success.

Reflection and Practice—

• Positive Accountability—working with someone as your partner to remind you of your commitment on an agreed upon schedule.

• Accountability is a good thing.

• Build habits—it takes a while to build it into brain/muscle memory. Get started now. Do a little each day. Consistency!

• The toughest part of getting started... is getting started.

• Use Positive Accountability to achieve the known things and use a coach when you're stuck or need to define what you are looking for.

• Be intentional!

• Consider keeping a journal and reflect daily for just 5 minutes per day (see my November 1, 2014 Blog *Reflection is the key to personal growth.* roycewhite.com

Conclusion—

It takes two to conquer your goal when you don't have the tenacity or startability yet to do it on your own. It's okay (and wise!) to get someone to help you. Better to get someone to help and accomplish your goal now than to do it on your own and never get started—or worse—start and don't finish. Be willing and reach out to someone to help you accomplish this. Once you succeed, you have the win necessary to move on to doing it on your own.

You cannot change the past... BUT, *you* can change *now* to affect the future, and, by doing that, you can change the outcome of your entire life.

—◆—

— 2 —

How Do *You* Spell Success?

**"Success is not final, failure is not fatal; it is the
courage to continue that counts."**
— Winston Churchill —

**"If at first you don't succeed, try, try, again. Then quit.
No sense being a damn fool about it."**
— W.C. Fields —

Remember high school football games? The crisp fall air, the pep
band blaring in your ear, the smell of grass stain and sweat, the teams
battling for position on the field, the marching band storming the field
at half time, not yielding to the players, the cheerleaders... I remember
that one silly cheer—

"S.U.C.C.E.S.S.—that's the way we spell success, la-de-da..."
(okay—my sister was a cheerleader for five years so I heard it 200,000
times more than you did.... they are all burned forever in my brain...).

At least we made our grammar teachers happy. For many of us, that
is the way we spell it—meaning, we've never really thought about it;
it's just a nebulous, random, unattainable concept out there and we're
doomed to mediocrity the rest of our lives and we'll live in poverty
and die in squalor and... YIKES! It's affecting me!

I love the two quotes above on success. They exemplify the two extremes by which we live success. Winston Churchill reminds us that success is really more about being steadfast, and failure is not the sum total of our lives. On the other hand, W.C. Fields calls us to be quitters. Yes, he was just being funny, he was a comedian, but so many of us adopt this philosophy—"Oh I failed. Better go back to not trying so hard and just being a follower—I don't have what it takes." We don't say it out loud, but in our heart of hearts, we embrace the failure, heave a sigh, and return to mediocrity. Instead of failing *forward*.

My passion in life is to help other people discover and succeed at their passion—their calling... so *failing forward* means a lot to me. I don't want to see anyone give up when they DO have what it takes—they just need a push, some accountability, and just maybe, some coaching.

Why We Fail

Financially inept (don't understand what it takes financially to accomplish something). Incompetent. Tired (a lack of energy or emotion). Selfish. Physically unfit. Angry. Out of Balance emotionally, spiritually, physically, intellectually. Lack of knowledge. Lack of resolve. Lack of desire. No persistence. No tenacity. Unwilling to learn. Unpracticed. Didn't do the homework. Lazy. Lacking vision (I don't mean non-sighted, I mean not looking ahead). Lack of leadership. Low integrity. Not failing forward, but making the same mistakes—not learning from your mistakes. Plus a whole lot more.

The reasons why we fail are myriad, and one of the greatest ways to *not* fail, is to have someone around to inspire you, to lift your head, to hold your image for you when you falter. THAT's the *heart* of Positive Accountability. Interestingly, in the Psalms in the Bible, King David called God the "lifter of my head." Someone that lifts your head is someone who helps you when downcast, who helps you look at your problems, and deal with the situations—to move onward and upward. C.S. Lewis calls us to get up and get going—*"It may be hard for an egg to turn into a bird: it would be a jolly sight harder for it to learn to fly while remaining an egg. We are like eggs at present. And we cannot go on indefinitely being just an ordinary, decent egg. We must be hatched or go bad."*

An on-line definition of success that I like, *"the accomplishment of an aim or purpose."* It can be the accomplishment of anything.

What Does Success Look Like?

So what does success look like *to you*? I'm a believer in doing what needs to be done when it needs to be done (even though I don't do it some of the time [especially house work], I'm still a believer in it!). So put down this book and write on a piece of paper, the inside front cover of this book, type in your computer, post on Facebook—GET IT DOWN in writing somewhere—*your* definition of success—what does it look like to *you*? Writing it down will give you a much better shot at accomplishing it. Bunches of studies have been done that show writing it with your *own hand* increases the possibility of it being done. I'm serious. Very serious. Dead serious. Don't just read for knowledge. Read and *apply* the knowledge—that is how you succeed—*applying* knowledge.

Stop for a moment and write something down. You don't need to plan out every moment of the rest of your life right now, just one idea of what success looks like to you. Try to be as specific as possible. Let your conscious mind flow freely to the paper. You are not being graded for doing this so don't worry about it. Here's an example for me...

I want to be a great Poppi (granddad) to my grand kids. I want to visit them often (without being a burden on my kids), teach them how to have fun, how to be disciplined, how to think logically, how to communicate, how to kayak, how to backpack, how to love and be loved, how to have respect and be respected, how to achieve, and a whole lot more. I want to do this from today until they cover me with dirt. I want them to be able to say, Poppi taught me a lot about truth, life, and fun.

"If you are clear about what you want, the world responds with clarity."
—Loretta Staples

"The world steps aside for the man who knows where he is going."
—James Allen

Okay. Now it's your turn. I'll wait while you write it down... if you need a place to write it, there is a page in the back of this book (see the index in the back of the book, page 150) that has the title "My Definition of Success" (original, huh!). Jot something down there or in your journal. Change it when it changes. It will be fun (and profitable)to look back over time and see how it has changed or been added to. Remember to date your changes and additions.

(The Jeopardy song is *not* playing and there is *no* clock ticking—

take all the time you need...). Was that enough time? Okay—you know best....

Why Define Success

Success comes in various shapes and sizes. Why? Because *we* come in various shapes and sizes, tastes and hopes, and success is different for everyone. When we *talk* of success, we usually mean financial success. But it might be a gold medal at the Olympics, finding a good spouse, getting the last child out of the house (empty nest), starting a business, getting a degree from the local university, losing weight, learning to speak in public, ruling the world... We define success differently than others—and we define success differently for different things in our *own* lives.

Why is it important for us to define success in order to put Positive Accountability into practice? Because without a definition of success, without knowing what we really, really, really want to achieve, there is little power allocated to achieving it. If you don't have a purpose, there's no reason to do it.

Zig Ziglar, the great motivational speaker of the 1970s and 1980s, tells a wonderful story of Howard Hill, the greatest archer of the 20th century (maybe of all time). Howard won 196[20] consecutive archery contests. Howard could put an arrow dead center in the bull's-eye and split it with the next arrow (or at least chip the first—it's actually quite hard to split an arrow). He was amazing. He was in the 1938 *Robin Hood* movie with Errol Flynn—he was the archer that came in second after Robin in the great contest for the "Golden Arrow."

Zig said that he himself, although not a great archer like Howard Hill, was a good teacher, and if he spent an hour with you he could have you hitting the bull's-eye more consistently then Howard Hill... PROVIDED you first blind-folded Howard and spun him around a number of times. "That's ridiculous" you say—and you're right. Who can hit a target without seeing it?

Therein lies my point. You can't hit a target you cannot see. Neither will you hit your goal of success that you do not define. And if you don't define what success looks like to you, how will you know what to shoot at? And why get an accountability partner to help you hit a target that isn't there... This is one of the greatest reasons why people do not succeed (or don't even get started!)—because they haven't defined it. If you don't have a *stated* (and written!) goal of, let's say, hiking 25 miles a day for five days on a section hike of the Appalachian Trail or the Pacific Coast Trail, how will you know if you succeeded at your goal? Or a goal of saving $25,000 for a car in 36 months, or starting a new business, or FILL IN THE BLANK. If you can't see it, you can't accomplish it. It just makes logical sense.

So defining success, or defining any goal in life, gives you the clarity to take a worthwhile shot at it. Otherwise, you will just meander around, living life bouncing from one idea to the next, careening from one person to the next, wondering what you will be when you grow up (already being at age of 45) and never utilizing all the greatness you have been given. You're a dreamer, not an accomplisher. Many people talk—only 2% take action. Zig also reminds us about the seeds of greatness that are planted in each of us. It's up to each of us to cultivate those and grow into a valuable asset to ourselves, those we love, and the community at large.

Okay—you now know the reasons *why* to define success, so now let's talk about *how* you define it.

How to Define Success

One of the visuals I give to my coaching clients sometimes is this—
"Imagine you're 85 years old, sitting on your front porch rocking away. I want you to look back through your life and tell me what you see that you have accomplished."

This allows them to think deeply about what they WANT their lives to look like even though their life has not happened yet. Then I proceed to have them better quantify their accomplishments. For instance, being a musician and a leadership trainer, I coach a number of musicians and managers of bands. When one of the "accomplishments" the musician sees over the years is "play to a large audience," I ask how large that audience is. A thousand people? Ten thousand? Fifty thousand? It defines what they really see as their success.

For some, it's simply that they want to make enough money to do the things they want. Have a family, buy a house one day. Enjoy life. Don't need to "make a million dollars." That defines you also. For others, they see HUGE financial success, and, if they're serious about getting there, they have an enormous amount of work to do—you've got to *give up to go up*—and the higher you want to go, the more you have to give up. Make sense?

Seven Spheres of Life

In each of the seven major spheres of life, *spiritual, family, physical, career, financial, intellectual, and social* (some add creative, environmental, and emotional, but I think those are derivatives of these main seven), we should be defining success in each area so we know what we're about, what we're looking for, and whether we have found it. Let's take a look at some of these to give you an idea of how to do it. My examples are not sacrosanct—just showing you what type of questions to ask yourself. It's reflection time! If we don't reflect, we won't learn from what we already know and have experienced. Again, these are just examples. Ask yourself similar and varied questions.

Spiritual. What do I believe? Why do I believe that? Is this important to me? Is there evidence that supports that belief? If I do believe, what does that look like for me in life? Is it just there in case I'm wrong about life so when I die I have a safety net? Are you a polytheist, believing in many gods? A monotheist, believing in one god? An atheist, believing in no god? An agnostic, unsure if there's a god... What impact does this have on you? What constitutes your life being successful in this area?

If God is real, having success knowing God is important—possibly the most important thing you could know. If God is not real, then don't waste the time. But choose wisely. Error in this area can be catastrophic to your life.

Family. What does success look like to you? Married? Kids? Single? Don't wait for someone to come along that tickles your desire, determine what you want. May change over time, but know what success in family looks like. If you have a family, does success look like spending time with them? Nurturing them? Saving for college? Home schooling them? Teaching them? Getting them started in business? What is success in your family life?

Career. What does success there look like? President of the company? Starting your own business? Happy with being a great sales person? An engineer designing things for a large company? Singer/songwriter playing before tens of thousands of people? I love the quote that "people give up looking for a career the moment they find a job." [21]

Searching for a Job...

One of the things I coach people in is finding a new job. Here's a normal scenario for someone looking for a job—

• Search Monster.com or Indeed.com...
  • Scour the paper...
  • Ask friends and family...
  • Post on your Facebook page, tweet ad nauseum
  • Go to some interviews
  • Maybe get an offer
  • Take the job

That, in its entirety, is getting a job through an *employer's* perspective. Here's how you *should* do it—unless you're lazy and just want to get by and not have much responsibility or pay...

Sit down and define what success looks like to you as a career. RE-SEARCH and find the company YOU want to work for—don't just take what comes to you—YOU go to them! Not all companies are alike. Some are in the top 100 to work for, others will drive you batty and you will be gone in six months. Maybe three. Some have awesome opportunities for growth, great benefits, educational programs, fitness programs, good financial rewards, excellent leadership, and on and on. Find the BEST company to work with (again, unless you're just mediocre—than just go find a job) and start to pursue them!

Once you find the company, and you may find a few, put them in order, then send a letter to the president telling him that you are awesome in this field and you have researched their company and you want to work with them so you can bring your dynamic skill set to add to their powerful leadership and productivity to create even more opportunity and greater success for you and their company. As a CEO, I can tell you that would have gone to the top of the stack. At the very least I would want to see if you're anything of what you describe! (Note: the best read right now on getting hired is Dan Millers *48 Days to the Work You Love*—stellar book[22]).

My point here is to be uber proactive!! Don't just let stuff *happen* to you, get off your petoot and get going! Remember Albert Einstein's definition of insanity? *Doing the same thing over and over again and expecting different results.* If you continue to do the same thing—and that same thing is little or nothing, and thinking you will get different results—you're never going to get where you want to be.

So define what you really want in every case—don't just do it because you *have* to. Get your purpose straight and then fly like an eagle to it! Like one of my favorite mentors Scott Fay says, "What do you really, really, really want?" [23] Don't play with this. Take the time to figure it out—***DO THE HOMEWORK***. Then—you will succeed. But if you never define success, you will never succeed at it... and you won't need any accountability to help you get where you're not going!

A Glimpse of Working with Your Partner

Defining success is paramount to your future and to being able to ask someone to be your accountability partner. Imagine a conversation between your accountability partner and yourself when you DON'T know what success looks like...

Royce: "Morning David. I need some accountability on my career."

David: "Morning Royce. Great. Where do you want to go with it?"

Royce: "With what?"

David: "Your career."

Royce: "I don't want to go anywhere, I just want some accountability. This is an accountability partnership, you know."

David: "Yes I know. What do you want to achieve?"

Royce: "I guess I'm achieving what I want."

David: "What do you want?"

Royce: "I dunno. More money I guess."

David: "Okay, so you want me to hold you accountable to asking your boss for more money."

Royce: "WHAT?!? Are you trying to get me fired?"

David: (dial tone.........)

Without a goal or definition of success, there is nothing driving you to the place you want to go because you don't have a destination in mind! It's like Alice's conversation with the Cheshire cat in *Alice in Wonderland*—

"Would you tell me, please, which way I ought to go from here?" said Alice.
"That depends a good deal on where you want to get to," said the Cat.
"I don't much care where –" said Alice.
"Then it doesn't matter which way you go," said the Cat.

If you don't know which way you want to go, if you don't know what success looks like, it doesn't matter which way you go. You'll eventually get somewhere. You probably won't like it, but you'll get somewhere.

Now imagine you *know* what success looks like before the last scenario with David. The conversation now looks like this...

Royce: "Morning David. I need you to help me stay on target to apply with the CEO of MegaCompany International." (Specific!)
David: "Great—how often do you want me to check in?"
Royce: "Twice a week, normal time is good. Text me. I want to have a yes or no within 30 days."

Done. You know what you want and David is going to help you stay on target to get there. He's not a resource for information on HOW to do it, just my accountability partner to help me get and stay on target.

So knowing what I really, really, really want is paramount to my success. Without knowing, I'm doomed to repeat history and work on other peoples terms. And you know what author, entrepreneur, and motivational speaker Jim Rohn says about that—

> "If you don't design your own life plan, chances are you'll fall into someone else's plan. And guess what they have planned for you? *Not much*." (Emphasis mine.)

Before you go into anything, define what success looks like for it. Even if that changes over time. Give yourself a target to hit. A goal to reach. By accurately writing out what success looks like for you, it defines the rules for everything and everyone and how they need to play along in order to be included in the story—including you!

If you don't do it now, you probably won't do it. As a matter of fact, I got $10 that says you won't do it if you don't do it now—at least not until you read this again, get sick of not accomplishing, or read something else that says something similar. It's the *Law of Diminishing Intent* which says, *"The longer you wait to do something you should do now, the greater the odds that you will never actually do it."* Booyah.

It's the end of the chapter—a great stopping point to take the time to write down your definition of success...

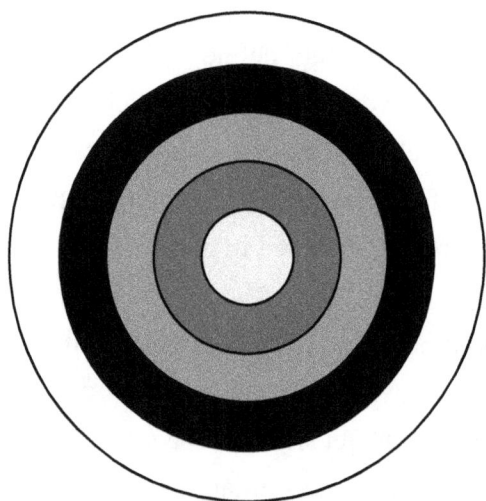

Reflection and Practice—

• Success is something that is individually oriented. No one else can define success for you. You must take the time to define it for yourself. In fact, don't let anyone else define it for you!

• Success is like a blindfolded archer who can't hit his target. If you can't see your target, you can't hit it. Further, you don't even know which way to shoot. If you define it, you know where you're going and have a great chance of hitting it.

• Defining success and goals gives you the clarity you need in life to take your best shot.

• Ask yourself a lot of questions and be curious about your hopes and dreams. Where do they all point?

• Knowing the *7 Streams of Life* and knowing where you are in them and what you want to achieve in them will help you define success.

Conclusion—Knowing *your* definition of success is critical because without it, you cannot really know the depth of the direction you want for accountability or life. Take some time and define it and write it down! *Write it down*!!! (Did I mention to write it down?)

> *"Give me a stock clerk with a goal, and I will give you a man*
> *who will make history. Give me a man without a goal,*
> *and I will give you a stock clerk."*
> —JC Penny

— 3 —

Self-Starter or Self-Finisher??

"Welcome every morning with a smile. Look on the new day as another special gift from your Creator, another golden opportunity to complete what you were unable to finish yesterday. Be a self-starter."
— Og Mandino —

"I do not have superior intelligence or faultless looks. I do not captivate a room or run a mile under six minutes. I only succeeded because I was still working after everyone else went to sleep."
— Greg Evans —

Self-Starters. Everyone is a self-starter. Well, 99% plus of us. We get up in the morning. We go to bed at night. We make our meals. We go to work. We pretty much all *start* things... For most of us, the problem is finishing them. It's not the self-starter that we admire, it's the self-*finisher*. For some reason, we erroneously call self-finishers, self-starters. Maybe we are talking about people that self-start the *hard* things in life—beyond the easy things of life—like a business, rigorous sports, or physical training (PT). Or maybe the Marines... or anything big...

We praise the *self-starter* entrepreneur because she had the guts to take a risk and step out and "start" a business. Of course we also bemoan that within 60 months, she's got a 50% chance of closing.[24]

Only 13% of those that *think* about starting a business actually start one. Maybe that's why we call them *self-starters*. Those that do the hard thing and step out to accomplish when the rest of us stay put, in the air conditioning, TV, video games, chips and salsa, bon-bons....

In fact, they are convicted strongly to reach a goal and know that the only way to get there is to get started—again my fav quote of my dad's, "The toughest part about getting started, is getting started." While I totally agree with that point, it seems sometimes that the harder part is to keep going when times get difficult—when you just feel like throwing in the towel.[25] But granted, without getting starting, there's nothing to keep working on!

Your Brain *Wants* to Get Started

On the *John Maxwell Team* (JMT), we have a mantra, *"Jump and build your wings on the way down"*—and it's right on target... Research from Russian psychologist Bluma Zeigarnik and from Kenneth McGraw shows that we are better at remembering things that are partially done vs. completed. Zeigarnik tested the memory of people doing simple brain tasks like puzzles or crafts. Then, the researchers interrupted them and asked them to recall with specific detail the tasks that they were doing or had completed.

Zeigarnik found that people were twice (two times) as likely to recall more detail about the tasks they had been *interrupted* during than in the tasks they had actually completed. That's significant. Similarly, In a study by Kenneth McGraw, participants were given a very difficult puzzle to solve with an unlimited amount of time to solve it. ALL of the participants were interrupted before they could finish, and then told that the study was over. Done. Complete.

Despite being told they were done, nearly 90% of participants continued working on the puzzle anyway. 90%! That's basically—statistically just about everyone!

These studies show us that when people finally get started, they are *much* more inclined to remember the task and finish it. Our brain is actually made to handle the expectations of the huge workload of an upcoming task. After starting a task, your brain *wants* to finish it.

The *Zeigarnik Effect* and the McGraw study show that the best way to get finished—or the best way to accomplish—is to get started doing something. Anything.[26] Start your diet. Begin writing your book. Advertise your coaching. Network for your speaking. Start connecting. Jump already—that's definitely starting…

Again, from my favorite book, *The 15 Invaluable Laws of Growth*, John Maxwell quotes Harvard psychologist Jerome Bruner who said, "You're more likely to act yourself into feeling than feel yourself into action."

To overplay a phrase—just do it. Be intentional and do it. Today. Now.

Million Dollar Loss

It was April 12, 1996. *My* day that has lived in infamy. I went in to work early as usual, though, like the past several weeks, I had been up all night trying to see how to salvage the company. Because of a sudden world-wide shortage in product, and a bad decision on my part, the company had lost nearly a million dollars in the space of a couple of months.

It was just 5 short years since I started the company. Sales had doubled every year. We were sitting at 5 million in sales with a great new idea and a million dollars in advertising placed and running to ensure our success. We had 45 excited, exceptional team members ready to soar into the next segment of growth. We were on our way to doubling this year also. I literally had an offer every three weeks from some competitor or investor to buy the company. Things looked really good.

Then, the bottom fell out. We couldn't get the bigger quantities of product to sell that we had planned—we couldn't even get what we *were* getting.

On that fateful morning, I had assembled the entire team in the conference room to share the news. We couldn't afford to keep all of the team, and the remaining staff would have to take serious cuts to survive—if it was even salvageable. I had to cut 35% of the staff and my heart felt like breaking.

After I shared the news, I broke down and fell to my knees. Here were my friends, my family, people that had followed me into the battle to build something from nothing. I had let them down, and for many of them, I had to let them go. I wept there on my knees in front of my family and friends. I had failed. They gathered around me and prayed for me. I wept some more.

Failure is an event, not a person (Zig Ziglar).

Then the most amazing thing happened. Those that I let go, had an incredible attitude about them and were thankful for the opportunity. The opportunity? They went about finding new jobs quickly so as not to be a burden on the company. What???? Those that remained had a renewed energy to find a solution, a way to increase sales in spite of the problem. What an incredible team.

The moment had been so powerful and so renewed my strength, that I committed then to do all that was in my power to work it out. We determined NOT to go into bankruptcy. We also decided to call every one of our vendors and tell them of our troubles and ask them to work with us. We called about 80 vendors and told them of our plight and pleaded with them to work with us and promised them we would pay our debts to them no matter how long it took.

They were all willing to work with us. Every last one. Some begrudgingly, but still willing. It took almost five years to pay it all back, but we did. And it made us much stronger. I remember one vendor to whom we owed the most money. He was also the one to receive the final payment. He was so thankful and couldn't believe any company would work so hard to meet its obligations.

We also found a new way to make more money with less product, and grew the company in a much more efficient way.

Best selling financial author Charles J. Givens said, "Use the losses and failures of the past as a reason for action, not inaction." So often we are paralyzed by our failures. Givens father, a construction company owner, deserted the family and left them poor. This affected Givens mentally. In a 1989 interview, Givens said he once considered himself a "loser," and at 16 wrote a suicide note. In the late 1980s, Givens built a multimillion-dollar empire. Failure was an event, not a person.

Time will fail me if I recall the countless stories of those rising out of the depths of failure and despair, like Edison, Disney, Lincoln, the Wright Brothers, Beethoven, Steven Spielberg, Churchill and more. I'm sure you have your own story of failure and loss.

Finishing...

17 years later, I closed the doors to the company because the industry we were in had pretty much gone away. So it was a good run. Tough times... good times. Failures, successes, profit, loss.

The point is that *sometimes* it was harder to keep it all going—but we kept going in spite of it all. I started the company in my "basement" and I closed it in my basement—with a whole lot of building, traveling, marketing, managing, sales, hiring, production, financing and such in-between. So I self-started *and* self-finished it with an enormous amount of amazing help in between. I had some of the greatest team players any company has ever had.

In this case, although self-starting was tough, self-finishing was tougher. Had I been a part of a Positive Accountability group for CEOs, I would have done much better. I would have grown much faster and better. I would have been steered away from some bad decisions and bad actions on my part. The counseling would have been indispensable.

Another thing to do at the beginning of any serious project, is get a *Board of Directors* (or Advisors) set up. Not official Directors (unless you're a corporation), but one that acts like one—maybe just a couple of friends. They are your group of counselors—and wisdom is found in many counselors. They can steer you away from danger. You don't have to listen to them, you can always decide to plow ahead your way—which sometimes is the better way—sometimes... but they may just stop you from imploding. It won't hurt and can save you a lot of pain.

We typically don't go get help until after we're in trouble. We try to do it on our own instead of really calculating (budgeting) what it will take to get it done, believing we won't need help. Then we get in trouble and call for help after certain things have been messed up. Or don't call at all and simply give up. There's no reason to go it alone with the plethora of willing and able folks around to lend a hand.

A Christmas Story

I remember putting up Christmas lights on the outline of the house, second floor, outside. I pulled out the 40' extension ladder. It's two connected sections of 20' that you slide upward and latch at one foot intervals. That was tough enough by myself. I had kids coming over and I wanted the place to look homey and Christmassy for them. I then stood the ladder up against the house where I was going to start stringing lights. That was next to impossible and I almost lost it a couple of times. The top was still about 8 feet from the height I needed, so I pulled on the "extension" part of the ladder and raised it up another 8 feet. Voila. Hit the gutter at the top.

I loaded up with lights and climbed the ladder. Fairly stable. When I got to the top I started putting the end of the lights at the starting point, but then the ladder started to slide on the gutter. Frantically, I grabbed the gutter and pulled myself—and the ladder—back to a straight position. After pushing my stomach back down my throat to its rightful place and stopping my body from shaking (whew!), I quickly climbed down the ladder and got some help from my son Christian (thanks bud). He held the ladder for me and thereby saved me *and* his meal ticket. He's no dummy... and a great actor.

So why in the world did I think I could do this without help? It was clearly more than I *should* be doing alone. In my zeal to get it done, I forgot to take the time necessary to ensure I was doing it properly and safely. We do things like this all the time and many times with more dire consequences. We love to do the first thought we have without taking into consideration the necessary requirements of the task. We take unnecessary risks—especially guys. It's in our makeup.

Holly Green of Forbes puts it best—"Our brain doesn't like information gaps, so we tend to jump at the first answer/solution that looks good rather than take the time to examine all the data. This is especially true in a world where we receive more information every day than we have time to assimilate. Finally, our brains love to see patterns and make connections. This trait serves us well in many ways as we move through the world. But the brain doesn't always get it right."[27]

Ask for Help

Had I asked Christian for his help earlier, I would have not strained my back and been finished much more quickly. I actually ended up hurting my foot and I didn't finish putting the lights up. It's the same with Positive Accountability. Instead of waiting until you fail at something and have a negative situation, get someone to help you get on and *stay* on target from the beginning!

My goal was to get the lights up. I failed at that—or at least partially failed. I only got half the lights up. Next year I am calling my buddy Steve and asking him to come over for a couple hours and help me get them up. I'll throw in some steak chili and a Leffe Abby Ale at the end to pay him for his help. Not that he wouldn't help for free—it just tastes really, really, really good and I'll take any excuse for chili.

It's the same with Positive Accountability. Once you decide to do something, get someone to help you stay on target. Had I enlisted Christian from the start, I would have gone faster, not hurt myself, been safer, had a backup, and most importantly, I would have finished my task and reached my goal. And that's what I really wanted to accomplish.

You would be amazed at the number of people that quit just before they reach their goal. We get tired. We get discouraged. We get frustrated. We get—pick a negative emotion and FILL IN THE BLANK. But what if we have someone to encourage us along the way? A cord of three strands is hard to break.

With Positive Accountability, you take the time to get the help you need to finish what you start, and if you don't realize it at first, put it into place as soon as you *do* figure it out. Unfortunately, most of the time when we fail we just stop doing it because we are discouraged. This is when Positive Accountability does it's best work. When I get discouraged, there is someone to bring me back on track—just by checking in and reminding me that I had a goal that I wanted to accomplish.

"You don't drown by falling into water. You only drown if you stay there." (Edwin Louis Cole). Granted, sometimes it's good to stop throwing good money (or time) after bad and to abandon the goal. But for the most part, it was a good decision in the first place—it's just a matter of tenacity—sticking to it—that was needed to *get er done.*

We're going to learn to be self-starters. First, we are going to work with somebody as an accountability partner. Then, as we learn more how to succeed, we will move from needing a partner, to being able to do it ourselves. It may happen right away for some of us. Or it may take a long time. But that's okay because we will use accountability partners in the meantime. For a slew of reasons, we have trouble achieving on our own—but the more we actually start something and achieve it, the more we will be impressed to do it again. The only difference is that we have someone to help keep us on target in the beginning, which, again, is better than not doing anything at all.

Finally, maybe we will achieve naturally, but it takes us a lot more time to get there than it should. Positive Accountability will help us achieve in a timely manor, instead of waiting until we are 63 and we finally decide it's now or never. I don't have enough time (or patience) to for that. It's much more time and cost effective to accomplish it sooner than later. If I'm going to do it, do it now.

Reflection and Practice—

• Only about 20% of us are true self-starters. Self-finishing is the key.

• Get help to get and stay focused. Remember the story of my past business and of putting up the Christmas lights.

• Get the tenacity to stay on target even if it is sometimes harder than self-starting. Chapter 7 tells you how to *get* tenacity—to stay on target.

• If you start something that requires the help of an accountability partner, but fail to put one in place, do so as soon as you realize you need to have a partner. Best to do it in the beginning planning stages.

Conclusion—

We want to be self-starters and self-finishers. AND, we can get help along the way at any point from the very start to the very end. Sometimes we just need someone to help us up. Get help before you get into trouble. Get it when you start.

—ᨍᨍ—

— 4 —

Balance: The Wheel of Life

**"What is joy without sorrow? What is success without
failure? What is a win without a loss? What is health
without illness? You have to experience each if you are
to appreciate the other. There is always going to be
suffering. It's how you look at your suffering, how you
deal with it, that will define you."**
— Mark Twain —

*All work and no play makes Jack a dull boy. All play and no work
makes Jack a poor boy... All play and all work make Jack an exhaust-
ed boy. No work and no play—Jack be dead...*

Balance. Sheesh. It seems to elude us constantly. At least, it does me
and most of the folks that come to me for coaching and everybody I
know. Other than that...

Those that seem to have their *stuff* together look pretty good in the
balance department (maybe that same 20%) from Chapter 1 and 3 that
are self-starters). Why? Because good balance is part of having your
stuff together. If you're bad at loving and spending time with your family but excel at work, you don't have your stuff together—you haven't
been there, you haven't done that, you shouldn't get the tee shirt.

Think of balance in other areas. Riding a bike. Lean too far to either side and you fall over. Ride a motorcycle? Sitting at a stop light looks pretty cool and comfortable—when it's balanced. Lean too much to one side and that *Harley Heritage Softail Classic* will start pulling Gs with it's 750 pound carcass dumping you straight to the pavement. (I will neither confirm nor deny that I have experienced this.)

How about a balance beam in gymnastics? The *Beam Queen*, Nadia Comaneci from Romania, was the first female gymnast to be awarded a perfect score of 10 in an Olympic gymnastic event.[28] An amazing performance. I remember watching it on TV in 1976. A perfect 10. Anything out of balance and your score is shot—and you may even fall.

What happens when our equilibrium is out of whack? *Otitis interna* (Internal otitis) is an inflammation of the inner ear.[29] What causes it is rarely diagnosed, but it is believed to come from a viral infection of the *vestibular labyrinth* (naturally), which is the part of the inner ear that gives us balance. Dizziness, vomiting, and other nefarious symptoms can put you down during this infection. Our bodies don't like being out of balance, and when they are, our lives are miserable.

So it goes with the emotional aspect of our life, too. If our finances are tanking, we fear we'll be out on the street. If our relationship with family is strained, we are angry and hurt and we want to run from the problem (especially men). No friends? *Woe is me* comes into play.

In each case we aren't functioning *fully* as we should, and quite possibly, we are *way* off. Think of a car only running on a half its cylinders—low power, wasting half it's energy (gas), and washing down the walls of the cylinders which promotes premature ring and wall wear. Can we function? Yes, but for how long? Many times we won't care how we do in other areas when we are just concentrating on getting through this pain area—this *hunger spot.*

Right Time on the Right Things

So why is balance important to *Positive Accountability*? Because, like knowing how you define success (Chapter 2), the proper balance will help you make sure you are spending the right time on the right things. Why on earth would you want me to help you spend more time at work when you're already spending 80 hours per week there? That's not to say you shouldn't have an accountability partner for work, but, likewise, you should have a partner to help you spend the necessary time at home, and in other areas, too. Those things that you are weak in will hold you back much more than you realize.

You Get to Do Life Over!

In Kevin Hall's wonderful book on words, *Aspire,*[30] he tells the story about Dr. Gerald Bell, a professor at the University of North Carolina in Chapel Hill, and one of the world's most respected human behaviorists, and how Dr. Bell studied the lives of 4,000 retired executives with an average age of 70. Dr. Bell had asked them one question:

If you could live your life over again, what would you do differently?

The number one answer? *I should have taken charge of my life and set my goals earlier.*

Notice the major active part of this is "taken charge of my life," and they would do that by *setting their goals earlier*. Had they been more serious about the direction of their lives at a younger age, they would have accomplished much more—in every sphere of their lives, and been in a better place today (or at the time of the interview anyway). This is fleshed out more by the other nine top answers to that one question Dr. Bell asked them (we'll take a look at that in a moment).

DON'T MISS THIS!!! So many people read this study and say, "mmmmm." 4,000 business leaders toward the ends of their lives overwhelmingly cited that they *should have* taken charge of their lives and set goals earlier in their lives—which I think means earlier than they did. What does this mean for you? Be specific. Reflect significantly on this. Maybe stop reading for a few minutes, go to your quiet thinking place, and think on it... maybe even reflect on your own life and journal or take some notes of your thoughts.

If they had started saving and investing earlier, they would have compounded much more financially. Had they paid more attention to their intellectual needs, they would have done better in school and had more to use in life and career. Had they invested more time with their family, they would have built better relationships with their kids and spouse and have passed on more of the important things in life to them. All the important areas of their lives would be better—all the important areas would be compounding *positively* for them now instead of adding little or no value at all—or maybe even regressing. By letting life run them instead of them running life they limited their success—they were their own worst enemy.

Can't Balance My Check Book

When I graduated high school I didn't know how to balance my check book—and for graduates today, it's worse because everything is done online, and a lot of people don't balance—they just spend, spend, spend (credit card), hoping that the need to pay it back won't catch up with them. Of course you can use mint.com,[31] which will help you greatly, and I strongly suggest you check it out, but I digress... want to learn how to have great balance? Read on...

In high school and college, probably until I was 30, I didn't know anything about budgeting, planning, time management, personal growth, people skills, and a lot more. In short, I knew a lot of stuff about music, marketing, and other areas I studied or was gifted in, but had gapping holes in my life's "balance"—holes that would cause me to bleed out in many ways over the next 15 years. Had I had an understanding and practice of these things, it would have changed my life for the better over those years and protected me from unintentional self annihilation so many times. But life was for living, not for saving, investing, planning... *Let us eat and drink; for tomorrow we die...*[32]

I now have a mantra that I share with anyone that will listen and especially young people. "If you do these three things, you will be generally happy 95% of your life" (okay—you can't control everything). Some take it to heart, others just say, "That's nice." I won't bore you with this... Okay. I will bore you later in another chapter, or maybe another book because it's not boring, it's awesome and can make us enormously productive and successful. It actually has to do with taking charge of your lives at the earliest age possible as Dr. Bell discovered. But first I have to determine how to convince people to do it before I share it so they will take it to heart and move it to practice—albeit, I guess that's what I am doing in this book right now. Okay—I will tell you at the end of the book...

I couldn't find a study on when a person takes control of their life, but I am going to speculate, or maybe just take an educated guess here for informational purposes. I'm still looking for the study, and hopefully one day I will post an errata sheet to my website (errors, corrections, and other musings on a printed work) at

http://www.roycewhite.com/pa-errata/

Check it out from time to time for corrections, comments, and the like as I get more growth on the topic.

Today, 2014, we're getting married older (average age 30) and we're living at home longer (average age 24-27). The indicators here are that we don't have a job, or have a poorly paying one and are forced or choose to live at home with mom and dad.

Here are some indices of increasing responsibility or "Taking Control." Not that we *are* taking control at any point; we may just be *doing* these things.

What indicates to you that you are taking control?

• Scheduling your time
• Budgeting your money
• Getting a job
• Moving out (buy or rent a place, move in and rent with friends)

- Getting married
- Having kids
- Investing
- Starting a business
- Advancing career
- Paying for college

Again, we're not necessarily taking control just by doing these things. Taking control means being intentional about these things. It means pursuing a career vs. having a job; moving out to buy your own place or to give your parents the space; getting married because you are in love and want to share your life with this other person; having kids to bring up good people to help the world and your society; investing because you know it's the right thing to do to make it so you are not a burden on anyone in later years and to pay for the necessary things of life; intentionally starting a business or advancing your career to take life by storm and provide for your family better, and to be able to help others and not just letting it all "happen" to you.

So the answer is (whoa—*the answer is!* better take notes...) when you decide to live life intentionally—*that* is when you are taking control of your life. When you are doing anything *for a reason*—preferably a good one. Intentionality is such an important topic. When we set our hearts and minds on growing to the next level and ultimately to the top level, we are intentionally moving through life. Intentionality is the first law of John Maxwell's great book *The 15 Invaluable Laws of Growth*, and on it, I think, hinges all the other 14 laws. The book is my favorite read to give to people that want to take control of their lives, and I recommend it to everyone—even if they already have great control of their lives.

Survey Says...

Back to the survey... Here are the rest of the answers from Dr. Bell's single question, with the related sphere of life influence (page 34) after it in parentheses—

"I would have"
2) taken better care of my health (physical)
3) managed my money better (financial)
4) spent more time with my family (family)
5) spent more time on personal development (intellectual)
6) had more fun (social)
7) planned my career better (career)
8) given more back (spiritual)

Each of those items (answers) ties in almost perfectly with one of the seven major spheres of life I mentioned in Chapter 2 (see page 34). That means that they would have emphasized the important or major areas of life more—they would have done these things in order to be more balanced—for there's no reason to do them more if they had done them enough the first time around.

When we work too much and play or love too little, we create *hunger spots* in our life that are constantly gnawing at us to feed. Likewise by playing too much and not working enough. By not feeding them, we grow more agitated and start to make mistakes in other areas as well.

I remember a story, don't remember where it came from, about a mother whose two boys would be playing nicely together each morning, but then would start to get angry and agitated with each other, and finally break into a full blown fight. She would stop them, send them to the bathroom to go potty, and all life would be great again. This happened almost daily.

The point is they didn't want to stop playing, so even though they had to *go*, they just kept playing and didn't realize that the antsy nature they were adopting came from not relieving their bladders and so the antsy nature led to intolerant behavior and finally war, mayhem, and death... (okay—maybe not war...). *Out of balance.* (Note: I'm NOT saying that every incident of sibling rivalry (or even many or most) is caused by full bladders—it was just a great example of my point.)

When you look back at things that have happened in your history, you look with the worry taken out, so you have a much more balanced look at the situation. No instant gratification is taking place because you're looking back to something that was—not something that might be or is. It's a fairly balanced look. Further, when *asked* by someone else to look back, vs. looking back ourselves because a memory in our head was tripped from some extraneous situation (which can cause emotive aspects), we typically look back more thoughtfully—because there is *someone* there—the person asking—to hold us... accountable.

Being well balanced allows you to put your priorities in place and concentrate on the greatest area of weakness. As you will learn when you study leadership, specifically *The 21 Irrefutable Laws of Leadership*[33] by John Maxwell, you can grow to be a Level 5 leader *only* when you embrace all 21 principles, and not just major in a few. When you are weak in certain necessary areas, it will hold you back. Balance.

Likewise, when you are out of balance in life, it will keep you from attaining the highest levels of productivity in the areas you are good at because the problem areas are constantly pulling you down—whether you think they are or not. Your subconscious is dealing with all kinds of issues that are taking valuable processing time, hormones aren't giving you their best—it's a mess on the inside EVEN when on the outside everything looks calm, cool, and collective.

Fighting with your spouse or family will keep you from the concentration necessary to be at your peak in your work or play. "Nonsense" you say. "I can function to my fullest even when I am fighting with family." Sorry. Doesn't work that way. Our mind plays the problems over and over in our subconscious, bubbling them to the surface (consciousness) from time to time.

Science Daily noted a study of what happens when we get angry.
"When we get angry, the heart rate, arterial tension and testosterone production increases, cortisol (the stress hormone) decreases, and the left hemisphere of the brain becomes more stimulated. This is indicated by a new investigation that analyzes the changes in the brain's cardiovascular, hormonal and asymmetric activation response when we get angry."

"Inducing emotions generates profound changes in the autonomous nervous system, which controls the cardiovascular response, and also in the endocrine system. In addition, changes in cerebral activity also occur, especially in the frontal and temporal lobes," Neus Herrero, main author of the study and researcher at UV, explains." [34]

*En Inglés, por favor...*You don't need to fully understand all that to figure out there are so many things going on that you don't realize (or understand) that can keep you from your best.. We all love to think we are in total control of ourselves, but it just isn't so. Those hormones cause a lot of problems and you can create a lot of havoc at work or elsewhere while this is going on ("Don't Drive Angry!" [35]).

Contrast being well balanced and the effect it will have upon your day. If you are happy, content, and not concerned about a major problem, finances, etc., you function better in your other tasks—you don't have to concentrate as hard to succeed—you can use the extra effort to be creative and improvisational.

This is why you want all your functions in muscle memory—meaning you've done them so many times it's natural. Once something is out of the conscious effort into subconscious effort, it's in muscle memory, and that frees your conscious mind to spend the time once used for the function for bettering it, improvising, or emphasizing something else. So even if you *are* angry or out of balance, you can still accomplish things. Special forces do it all the time. Olympic gymnasts do it all the time. Medics, like my daughter Stephanie, do it all the time. Though not for too long and not without consequence.

Here are a couple of real examples I have seen of how muscle memory puts you on the top of your game—

Lead singers in a band. If you don't know your lyrics backwards and forwards, inside out, upside down, sideways and completely, especially if you also play an instrument (which you will need to play flawlessly also while singing), you CANNOT concentrate on *connect-*

ing with your audience and being a good *frontman*—the number one problem in young bands and the number one thing you need to do, according to live performance coach, Tom Jackson. This WILL keep you from building fans and getting ahead in your musical career. If you know your music, lyrics, and instrument so you can play in your sleep or while dead, you can then concentrate on *connecting* with your audience and making moments—the key to building a fan base.

Salesperson. If you don't know the product, you don't know the benefits, the features, etc., in your sleep, you cannot concentrate on the customers body language and word usage to see what her real objections are. If you study your product(s), know them inside out, their flaws, their greatest strengths and weaknesses, and all the policies related to them—I mean you live and breathe these things—you are free to be creative in your sales and be present in the moment to listen intently to the objections and questions, and truly further the sale. This won't make you a great sales person if you don't know how to sell, but couple this with great sales technique and understanding and you will soar!

Leader. If you know by heart the 21 Laws of Leadership, the The 17 Indisputable Laws of Teamwork, the 7 Habits of Highly Effective People, etc., then the information works from your subconscious mind to your conscious mind and you don't have to wonder what to do when the concept is needed—you know what to do. This frees you to be creative in your leadership and test new things, to listen intently, to see what your team really thinks and guide them more effectively to the goal. If you don't do the homework, you won't get the grade—or worse, you fail.

Muscle memory is paramount for being *great* at anything. Anything. Even if you're gifted, maybe ESPECIALLY if your gifted. Many times, gifted people rely on their gift and don't work and push to grow their talent and, hence, never achieve full greatness (gifted under-achievers). You have to get it into "automatic" so you can concentrate on improvisation that is effective and adds a greater experience for all. This is accomplished though repetition—learning it and practicing it.

"This is common sense" you say. Yes it is—but as the great mentors have said too many times to count, "common sense isn't common practice."[36] We need to make the effort to make it common practice. What does that take? Positive, purposeful, pragmatic accountability.

If I stopped right here and you made the effort to do the above and nothing else, you would be awesome at what you do. Holding on to that awesomeness is another story, and also one of the main aspects of Positive Accountability.

The Wheel of Life

The Wheel of Life is just that—a wheel, or circle, broken up like a pie chart into a number of different pieces. Each piece represents one of the streams of life I mentioned earlier (the original copyrighted version that you are about to see only has six streams, but you will get the point and can apply it to the seven streams). Why am I showing you this version instead of one with the seven streams? Because the one I am showing you is the original and I want to honor their copyright.

WHEEL OF LIFE®

TOTAL PERSON®

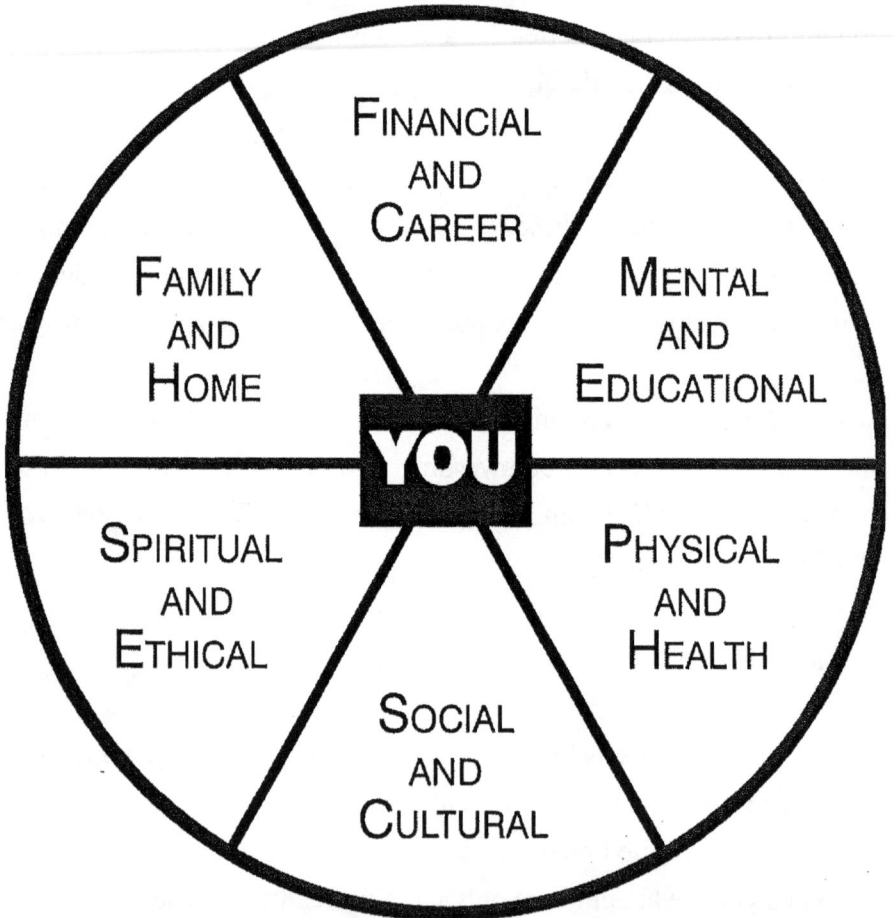

FINANCIAL AND CAREER

MENTAL AND EDUCATIONAL

FAMILY AND HOME

YOU

SPIRITUAL AND ETHICAL

PHYSICAL AND HEALTH

SOCIAL AND CULTURAL

WHEEL OF LIFE®

Copyright © The Meyer Resource Group, Inc.
ALL RIGHTS RESERVED
(Used with permission by The Meyer Resource Group, ® Inc.)

The following is the concept of the *Wheel of Life* and the actual wheel, used by permission. It's not how I explain it, but I want you to have an understanding from its creator's perspective...

THE WHEEL OF LIFE, *Copyright The Meyer Resource Group*

SETTING PRIORITIES IN ALL AREAS OF LIFE

You are a complex, unique individual. Part of your complexity stems from the fact that you fill many roles in life and you possess numerous needs and desires that grow out of your distinctive potential. Your needs and desires are best fulfilled by using your potential to be as productive as possible in your business pursuits. However, you will be more productive over a long period of time and you will find greater satisfaction in your accomplishments when you establish priorities in all six areas of life: Family and Home, Financial and Career, Mental and Educational, Physical and Health, Social and Cultural, and Spiritual and Ethical.

Enhance your performance and your enjoyment of life by keeping all areas of your personal and business life in proper perspective and by setting priorities in each of these areas of life:

1. Family and Home
Make your family and home life more rewarding by giving to it some of the energy you save through better organization at work. Spend quality time to maintain meaningful relationships with all members of the family. Exhibit the same caring for them that you do for the members of your team at work.

2. Financial and Career

Exercise the same careful watch over your personal financial affairs as you demand in your business. Consider the effect of finances on your ultimate career goals and priorities.

3. Mental and Educational

Continue to grow in knowledge of your career field and knowledge of the world in general. Read something every day that stimulates you to think about important ideas.

4. Physical and Health

Successful people take care of themselves physically; they know a healthy body supports an active and creative mind and turns stress into a motivating force for achievement. Set a high priority on eating nutritious meals, exercising, and getting enough rest to be as productive as possible.

5. Social and Cultural

Your relationships with people make life worthwhile. Develop a broad circle of friends with whom you have mutual interests. Remember also that the most successful people know how to get along well with others. In addition, they enrich their own lives and the lives of others by participating in cultural activities.

6. Spiritual and Ethical

Give attention to becoming the kind of person you want to be and to the values you want to demonstrate in your life. Give back to others some of the rewards and blessings of life that have been yours. Find some greater cause than yourself and support it with your time, money, and influence.

On page 70, you will find the actual *Wheel of Life* drawing. Copy it and do this exercise once every three to six months of your life to keep a check on where you are.

There are a number of variants to this wheel out there—some with, I think, good additives and break outs. I like the one that follows the 7 streams of life that I outlined in Chapter 2. Some add other areas, such as the *Life Assessment Wheel* by Chris Warnky[37]—a great coach, friend, and fellow John Maxwell Team member—which adds *Legacy, Character, Life Pace, Adventure* and variations of the main categories.

The key to all of these is that they are a tool, typically administered and analyzed by a professional coach, but which can be used by you to take your temperature at any one moment. But you must be brutally honest. This will tell you where you are out of balance and what you should spend some time correcting. What good is it to have a tire (wheel) on your car that is fine for 80% of the tire but low on one side—we call that a flat and it will still stop you from traveling until you change it. So it is in life. When we are out of balance in any one area, we are running on a flat and the rest of our life suffers.

It's like having a splinter in your big toe or thumb. The rest of you becomes very uncomfortable with that little pain on a very important spot—you can't walk well or pick things up correctly. In short, you are greatly hampered until the problem is removed—and if you don't fix it, it becomes infected, even to the point of losing the appendage.

Life problems are no different. If you don't fix them, they build up substantial problems in the area of lack (hunger spot) and can start doing additional damage to other areas of your life. Left untreated, it infects the rest of your life and eventually pulls you down to its lowest level. Yuck.

[LOL. When I finished writing this sentence, my youngest son, Christian, 20, came in with a *splinter* which needed to be removed from his finger. He was in some pain and fear of the coming surgery—the removal of the splinter. After we were done, he mentioned that he can take blows all day long with no problem while LARPing (**L**arge **A**rea **R**ole **P**lay as knights and swordsmen), but a little tiny splinter rendered him useless—like the Lion of Androcles.[38] Thanks for proving my point Christian! I guess I had better not write about guillotines...]

As a good friend of mine would say, balance is key to a *well done* life. Take the cue from the 4,000 retired executives that have specifically told us what to do to make life more meaningful. We truly can make changes now before we get to the same place they were and are sorry we didn't make a change.

Reflection and Practice—

• If we're terribly out of balance, we may *not* think we need account-ability.

• We can spend a lot of time working more on things we are *not* out of balance in, thereby exacerbating the situation.

• Getting it into muscle memory is an important part of achieving.

• Take control of your life—EARLY! (Remember the Dr. Bell study).

• Let's get in balance as best as possible. Use the *Wheel of Life* or just rate yourself on the 7 spheres of life on a scale of 1 to 10, 1 meaning needs a lot of work, 10 meaning you've almost mastered it! Concentrate on the areas of weakness, EVEN if the other areas appear to be the ones you WANT to work on. This will alleviate collateral damage and allow you to be more well rounded and everybody will be happier—meaning you, your family, your friends... do this right now before you do anything else... and be specific!

Conclusion—

Four thousand executives can't all be wrong! We must live intentionally if we are to gain the tenacity we need to succeed. Balance is the key to ensuring we accomplish all the things we need to equally. Sometimes, some things need to be emphasized more than others, but balance is paramount for overall happiness and success.

— 5 —

How to Practice
Positive Accountability

**"The thing that lies at the foundation of positive
change, the way I see it, is service to a
fellow human being."**
— Lee Iacocca —

Okay. You've waded through the reasons to embrace Positive Accountability. Stay with me. The other material we went through to this
point, was preliminary and probably more strategic. Now on to the
tactical—the actual process.

Smell the Freshly Baked Bread...

A few thoughts, cautions, and reminders before we dive in. You need
to want to do this. If you are already are a self-starter, consider using
this methodology to help those that are not—don't just smirk at them.

When we had kids, my bride, Jody, starting baking bread to give us
better ingredients to eat and to help out in the finance department (btw,
thanks babe...). Many times the bread fell, or was under cooked, or had
some other malady (forgot a crucial ingredient). But, in time, her bread

was consistent and delicious. The house would smell of fresh baking bread every single day.....mmmmmmm. What a great memory. She used to take it out of the bread machine and cut off the soft, rounded top piece, put a little butter on it and bring it to me... wow... heaven... Nirvana... It didn't get any better than that... well, actually it did.

Positive Accountability *will* work if you do it—just like baking bread will work if you do it. You may not be good at first, but in time, perfection comes. Be willing to commit to it so accomplishment will come in its time.

Finally—The Process!

Okay. Let's do it by the numbers. Get your pen and paper (or iDevice/computer) and write this down.

1. *Choose your topic.* i.e. Lose 25 pounds. Learn a language. Take a class at the local college. Start a business. FILL IN THE BLANK. Choose your topic. Simple enough. BE SPECIFIC and SMART. (S.M.A.R.T. Goals *Specific, Measurable, Attainable, Realistic, Timely*). Not "lose weight" but lose 30 pounds by December 31, this year. Have a one-year and three-year business plan ready in 30 days. Sign-up for Psychology 101 at Main Street Community College by July 15. Be specific. Write it down. Do it now.

2. *Give the topic what I call the "reasonability test."* Is this reasonable for me? Learning to speak Italian fluently in three months. Hmmmm... don't think so. At least not for me with all the other things I have to do. Maybe you're a linguistics expert, already speak 12 lan-

guages, got nothing to do for 90 days so this is a piece of cake. Even so... Is this reasonable for you? Not for me but for you? That's the reasonability test. If it is, keep going. If it is not, what does it take to make it reasonable? More time, smaller goal? More work? Restate your goal with the new criteria and re-ask the question—Is *this* reasonable? If it is, move on to #3. If not, go back again... repeat.

3. *Write the goal down in a complete paragraph*—preferably by hand in your journal. Do NOT *just* put it into memory. Get it on paper. Write it out in nice, complete sentences. We can pare it down later. Let a stream of consciousness flow. You should buy a journal or notebook to keep your whole journey documented. The more you have the information documented, the more you can go back and draw conclusions from different things and the more you will know for the next project. Calibrate your tools! What made it work, what made it fail. It will save you time and money in the future.

There are various studies out there about how handwriting (versus typing) triggers things in our brain and causes us to remember better and to have a higher chance of achievement. That's fine. But my point is that if you don't have it written down, you have no specific detail of what has priority and what really needs to be done when. I see clients going from serious procrastination and non-self starting, to being more effective in one week just by getting their action items visible.

There are many camps of thought like goal setting, vision boards, planners, etc. The bottom line is that in all cases, things are written down and guide your direction. You can remove, add to, and see what is important to you at any one time. Most people agree you need goals, and more importantly, actions items (you need both) to get to success. If you don't write it down, it can get lost. We've got enough problem with procrastination derailing us—"write it down..." I really cannot say it too much... get it into muscle memory.

4. *Make a poster, card, sign, etc. and post* above your computer, as your screen-saver, on your bathroom mirror (unless this is of a sensitive nature). The point is to put up reminders all over the place so everywhere you turn it reminds you to achieve. I can't tell you how many times I went into the pantry and got a cracker or something without even thinking about it. Not cheating, simply not thinking about it—force of habit (old). It *used* to be normal, but now it's off limits. I need reminders until I make it a—what? A habit. Whatever the topic is, come up with a good sign and post it around. Maybe even a card for your wallet or pocket.

5. *Find an accountability partner.* This person should be a peer, not a boss, not a spouse, not a subordinate, but a peer. Preferably of the same gender. Why? Because men are from Mars and women are from Venus and we have a hard enough time understanding each other and this will only work against you if you don't follow it—trust me on this one.

A friend, a co-worker, someone from church, the gym, a peer. If you cannot find someone, call me—I will find you one. Well, don't call me, email me. Actually, go to my website and click on the *Partnerships* menu item and then choose *Accountability Partner*. This is actually detailed in Chapter 9.

Finding the right person is important; although, if they turn out to be the wrong person, you can end it amicably and try again. But why waste time? Here is a good process to use for finding a good partner.

What to look for in an accountability partner. These don't have to be exact, but the closer you get, the better it will work.

• Someone of your gender
• Someone close to your age
• Someone of the same peer level
• Someone in your time zone
• Someone who shares the hours you are awake (5:00a – 10:00p?)
• Someone of your demeanor (introvert, extrovert, ambivert...)
• Someone that has a good work ethic
• Someone who is excited & willing to help you
• Someone of proven character

Let's look at each one and why.

Someone of your gender. As I mentioned above, in general and most of the time, women understand women better and men, men. After 36 years of marriage my bride, still looks at me, shakes her head, and I'm sure says to herself, "What hole did he crawl out from?" But I can talk to one of my buddies and we grunt and say, "Yea. That's right. You betcha. Totally. Ats-right." When staying with the same gender, we also make room for each other and are not worried about getting the wrong message across—"Is he flirting?" It's just common sense—so make it common practice.

Someone close to your age. Better chance of finding someone and probably most of your friends are around your age. I know this seems obvious and, well, it *is*, but if you can find someone older and wiser and *willing*, go for it. I love helping people of all ages do this, but then, as you surmised, I am committed to this concept...

Someone of the same peer level. Bosses may unintentionally look down on you when you fail (good ones won't) and you may be afraid to share with them, so this one doesn't work. If the person is under your authority, you may be able to convince them that you didn't need to comply. You need to be able to trust this person to see past your smokescreens and hold you... you got it... accountable. Bosses will do that, but not necessarily in the right way. Subordinates may be afraid to if you have a strong character. Peers are usually similar to us. With a spouse/significant other, there may be a problem working together from a personality perspective. Choose wisely.

Someone in your time zone. Again although obvious, it makes it easier to be available to each other at the right time. I work with some people in time zones with three hours' difference, and, although it's not impossible, it does make it harder. As long as they're in the earlier time zone, it's okay. Although I get up at 4:29a, that is my PT (physical training) and reading time for the next few hours. And then breakfast time with my bride (the most beautiful and wonderful woman in the world!). So make sure the time zone and time is compatible with availability.

Someone who shares the hours you are awake. Additionally, someone who has similar sleep patterns as you do. If you work fire and rescue or police, you work shifts. One of my best friends is a cop and works from 4:00pm until 1:00am, spends time with family until 2:00a – 3:00a and then sleeps until about noon. It's tough to catch him in his off hours, so I usually talk to him for a few minutes when he's chasing bad guys. If you work shift, someone with the same shift would be best. You get the idea.

Someone of your demeanor/personality. This is important. If you're strong willed, someone who can take what you dish out and return it in kind will help you the most. If your an introvert, someone who will treat you the same is best. You will respond best to someone who is kind and firm. If they are not kind, maybe you should suggest that you hold them accountable for being kind during the next season! Just kidding. Never suggest what they should work on, unless you are long time friends. Then it's your duty to tell them they have egg on their face. That's true love.

Someone that has a good work ethic. Again, though obvious, you want someone who has a great work ethic and understands what it takes to get things done—someone with tenacity.

Someone who is excited & willing to help you. Don't select someone that is not excited to help you in this. As it is, this is going to tax all you are to accomplish it. You need a willing ~~victim~~ partner. There are plenty of people that, like in the parable, say "yes I will" and then, no they don't. Find someone who likes this concept.

You can also find someone who you will reciprocate with. Meaning, you will be partners to hold each *other* accountable—usually for different things, but it makes a better use of the time. In a way, this is the best way to do it because it allows two people to accomplish more in almost the same time. As well, the very nature of the other person looking to you for accountability will help them be more accountable.

Someone of proven character. If you know someone of high character, you know that they will stay on target to help you stay on target. Of course, you could be reciprocating with one another—holding each other accountable, which is fine and lets you use your time better (see above).

In concluding this search, you're looking for... you *plus*. Someone that is very similar to you. Albeit, they may struggle keeping themselves on target, helping someone else is easier then trying to accomplish it on your own.

So now we have a partner, the topic of our goal, we know it's reasonable *and* achievable, and we're ready to get started.

6. *Fill out the ACCOUNTABILITY WORKSHEET* form here (two pages ahead) and then send it to your partner. You can also find it on my website at

www.roycewhite.com/positive-accountability-worksheet/

or under the menu item *Partnerships, PA Worksheet*. Or you can write up your own. Print it out, fill it out, give a copy to your partner, and away you go.

The next page is a sample worksheet and the page after is the actual worksheet. Copy as needed.

(sample completed worksheet)

ACCOUNTABILITY WORKSHEET

Accountability Partner 1: The person being held accountable:

Royce White

Phone #: _555-555-5555 x555_

Text #: _555-555-5555_

Email address: _swingdancer@swingdanceva.com_

Accountability Partner 2: The person holding you accountable:

Bubba Warrell

Phone #: _554-444-4444_

Text #: _554-444-4444_

Email address: _bubba201@gmail.com_

The Topic of Accountability:

Sell my car and pay off my debts by November 15, 2016.
I still have $15,000 of credit card debt and I want to be
out of debt by November 2016. I need you to check in with
me three times a week to help me not spend foolishly. TY!

Conclusion Date: (if not ongoing) _November 15, 2016_

When to hold accountable: (days and times)

Days: _Monday, Thursday, Saturday_

Times: _7:30am & 5:30pm_

Method of Accountability: (highly recommend Text)

❏ Phone ☒ Text ❏ Email ❏ In-person

Siged _Royce White_

Signd _Bubba J. Warrell_

© 2014 Royce White. www.roycewhite.com. All Rights Reserved. Please copy freely to use personally. This copyright line must appear on any use. For non-personal use, please see www.roycewhite.com/copyright

ACCOUNTABILITY WORKSHEET

Accountability Partner 1: The person being held accountable:

_____

Phone #:_____

Text #: _____

Email address: _____

Accountability Partner 2: The person holding you accountable:

_____

Phone #:_____

Text #: _____

Email address: _____

The Topic of Accountability:

_____

_____

_____

_____

Conclusion Date: (if not ongoing)_____

When to hold accountable: (days and times)

Days:_____

Times:_____

Method of Accountability: (highly recommend Text)

❑ Phone   ❑ Text   ❑ Email   ❑ In-person

Siged_____

Signd_____

© 2014 Royce White. www.roycewhite.com. All Rights Reserved. Please copy freely to use personally. This copyright line must appear on any use. For non-personal use, please see www.roycewhite.com/copyright

7. Now let's talk about how this works, what to emphasize, and what to avoid, etc. The real meat & potatoes of Positive Accountability.

As the person being *held* accountable, we'll call you PA1 for short, never forget the person helping you is doing it because they *want* to see you succeed. Never treat them badly or get angry at them if you fail. Even if they forget to call you. It's your life. If they continually can't keep up, say "Thank you, I appreciate all you've done, but I need to move on"—then find someone else. Never be a toad if they are failing you. But also, don't stay stuck in that rut. Be thankful that someone was willing to try. Most people will succeed. Be kind.

Likewise, for the people *holding* the PA1s accountable, we'll call you PA2, don't chastise your partner for not accomplishing what they need to. Yours is a job of encouragement and timely reminder—you're the stronger one in the group because you are not trying to accomplish what they are. You want the best for them and you are rooting for them and helping them, but ultimately it is their responsibility. At some point you may get so tired of them not accomplishing, you want to move on—hang in there just a little bit longer. As I pointed out in Chapter 1, it does take a long time to build a habit. So at the very least, hold on for a month.

So don't abuse each other—be kind and courteous to one another. Do not be judgemental. Together, figure out a better way to deal with it. Maybe text every day instead of every other day. Maybe PA1 needs some coaching for several months—someone who is trained in helping you get to where you want to go. You can find a life/confidence/ executive coach, who will get you to the next level, on my website, and then use Positive Accountability with an accountability partner after the coach gets you unstuck.

Also, for those being *held* accountable, PA1 folks, consider making yourselves available to others as a partner to help them achieve their goals. You can swap with your partner and help them, too, or you can sign up on my website and help others from there.

Obstacles

There are obstacles to achieving success in general, and specifically to Positive Accountability. I want to look at a few of them so you are aware of them and prepared to tackle. There are more than these four but use the principles learned elsewhere in this book, or do additional homework (yes, homework!) to get to your success.

Fear. It's hard to do things afraid. But that's exactly what you need to do. We're constantly reminding ourselves on the JMT (John Maxwell Team) to "Do it afraid!" Why be afraid? What's going to happen? Is somebody going to kill you? Is death on the line? Certainly you need to weigh the wise options, but don't let unhealthy fear slow you down. Here are some notable quotes on fear from the some of the top motivational, inspirational, and leadership folks in the industry...

"Everything you've ever wanted is on the other side of fear." —*George Addair*

"Too many of us are not living our dreams because we are living our fears." —Les Brown

"In order to succeed, your desire for success should be greater than your fear of failure." —Bill Cosby

"Men go to far greater lengths to avoid what they fear than to obtain what they desire." —Dan Brown

"I have learned over the years that when one's mind is made up, this diminishes fear." —Rosa Parks

"Do one thing every day that scares you." —Eleanor Roosevelt

Fear is a lack of trust. Either in yourself or someone/something else. There is no such thing as darkness—only the lack of light. So add light to the subject and conquer the fear. Get the knowledge you need. And if you cannot do it alone, take someone with you—like an accountability partner. They will help dispel the fear. Having someone else there makes our hearts glad and we can accomplish better.

Pride. Yep. That nasty little beast that kills a lot of things. You don't want anyone to know that you are not a self-starter so you read this book, maybe stop halfway through, or even finish it, and never get around to getting a partner. The truth is, most people are rooting *for* you to succeed—not against you. Don't worry about what others think—it's your life. Do what you gotta do to get where you want to go. Dr. Seuss noted, *"Be who you are and say what you feel, because those who mind don't matter and those who matter don't mind."*

Flippant. Whimsical. Nonchalant. I can handle it on my own... We feel we don't need help to accomplish. That may be true—and if it is—

awesome! So go do it. Put it together and accomplish it. Stop reading this book now and tackle it! Make it happen. Plan the work and work the plan (dog-ear the page first...). BUT, if you cannot, or find that you *do not*, get some accountability help and get the thing done.

Life is too short to be stuck not accomplishing and not getting to where you desire to be. You could have been there years ago—maybe decades ago. To be candid, I'm not concerned whether you can or cannot do it on your own yet, I just simply WANT you to accomplish it!!! Today!! Or ASAP. There are few things so wonderful as accomplishing your goals and moving forward in life.

"Whether you think you can or you think you can't, you're right."
—Henry Ford

Laziness. This is a tough one. It has many different faces...symptoms. We spend our days working, eating, cooking, cleaning, and then we simply want some time to "relax." That seems reasonable. Except when you hold that to the light of wanting to accomplish something else. So many times our desire for comfort outweighs our desire to get the *thing* we really want. Chapter 6 on trading freedoms talks about this. If we stay in our comfort zone, we will be comfortable, but not getting to where we really, really, really want to go. If you want to succeed, you have to trade the comfort of relaxation for the comfort of accomplishment.

"Luck is always the last refuge of laziness and incompetence."
—JC Penny

"Laziness is nothing more than the habit of resting before you get tired." —Jules Renard

"Laziness is a secret ingredient that goes into failure. But it's only kept a secret from the person who fails." —Robert Half

"Laziness never arrived at the attainment of a good wish."
—Miguel de Cervantes

There are many obstacles to success, but accept *none* of them. Set your heart and mind on the goal and stay glued to it until you're done. Then move on to the next one. And use legal, ethical, and wise methodology to achieve it. Your bag of tools should include Positive Accountability because it will almost always help you get there.

"We are built to conquer environment, solve problems, achieve goals, and we find no real satisfaction or happiness in life without obstacles to conquer and goals to achieve."
—Maxwell Maltz

Reflection and Practice—

• We hate to let people down so we will work to accomplish our task simply because someone is rooting for us.

• Timely, frequent contact will help us stay on target.

• Non-judgemental accountability—positive—will help people not despair when they fail.

• When I am held accountable, I have a tendency to succeed at my goal instead of having a tendency to fail at my goal.

• I know that it is ultimately up to me and I need to do it because I want to accomplish it. My partner is simply there to remind me of that.

Conclusion—

This is where the proverbial rubber meets the road. Finding the right person is important to your success. Not all encompassing, but important. Their task in holding you accountable is not huge or daunting, but responsible people make the best partners. Use the form and the definitions here to search for and find the right person to be your partner. Once you find someone, you both are well on your way to accomplishing more by helping one another. As well, if you cannot find someone or don't have the time to find someone, you can find someone from my website as mentioned earlier, and it's the whole topic of Chapter 9.

— 6 —

Accountability & Freedom

"It is wrong and immoral to seek to escape the consequences of one's acts."
— Mahatma Gandhi —

"When people say "If I only knew then what I know now" makes me wonder why they aren't using that wisdom now."
— Rob Liano —

Everybody hates being told what to do—unless you're looking for direction. But in that case you are getting what you want and merely getting input from others—so you're not really being told what to do. So why will accountability work if we don't like being told what to do??

Great question.

First, when we are involved in Positive Accountability, I'm not telling you what to do, I am reminding you to stay on target to something you *already* thought and agreed you wanted to accomplish. I am an interested party that wants to help you achieve your goal, and I want you to help me achieve my goal. There is a symbiosis (a relationship between two people or groups that work with and depend upon each other) that is happening to achieve the goals of each. As well, because *we* want to accomplish, we are happy to help *you* accomplish. When two people work towards the same goal to succeed at something (albeit different somethings), they are more apt to work together, helping the other stay on target. In this case, our similar goal is to succeed. We want to be accountable to be successful in some way.

Second, more to the point, we have a great tendency to feel that something that *organizes* takes away freedom, versus *gives* freedom. Sort of like an oxymoron or a contradiction—which are not the same thing.

You would be amazed at the number of people that think budgeting every dollar of your money takes away your freedom to spend as you desire. When, in reality, if you control all your money, it *gives* you more freedom to spend as you really want to. Why? Because if you don't budget, you'll be out of cash soon and in debt soon after, and debilitating debt after that. For a detailed explanation and a great understanding of debt elimination and wealth creation, see Dave Ramsey's *Financial Peace University*.[39] Read FPU, *apply* the principles, and you will save yourself a lifetime of heartache—really. Seriously.

When you fail to budget, you waste money. You don't know how you are spending and where it's all going. All you know is there are more bills than month.

My daughter Stephanie is the most amazing fire/medic. If you're hurt in any serious way, you *want* her to be the first responder. She will get you to the emergency room—alive. She is your best chance for survival. In 2006 she was a young medic with the county. She studied hard, went to the academy, passed her exams, and started practicing. She also had a brand new paycheck that was larger than anything she had ever seen. With salary and annuities, she was making good money.

At the end of one year, she asked me if I would help her do her taxes- it was her first time doing them alone. I has happy to help. Being a TurboTax veteran of 10 plus years, we tackled the forms for her favorite uncle.

"Looks like you owe about four grand," I said.
"WHAT?" she bellowed in her most commanding voice.
"I don't have $4,000 dollars."
"Well, file your forms and ask them for a payment schedule. They will contact you and set something up."

Having just finished her taxes, I knew exactly how much money she made and what she *didn't* spend it on—no house, no interest, no investments. Where did it all go? And it was a pile of money. Most did go to legitimate things, but all her extra cash and spending money was gone.

Not wanting her to repeat this scene next year, and feeling I had not given her all the necessary financial education she needed growing up in order to avoid this, we sat down to talk about where the money went and how to begin to budget. She didn't know. She couldn't piece it together. I told her to save every receipt and throw it in a box from now on. To make a long story short, she had a penchant for shoes, clothes, and eating out. I won't embarrass her by saying how much it was...

By not budgeting she didn't know where she was at any one time. She had no money with which to pay this additional bill from Uncle Sam. Or any other emergency that might come along.

Today, she has it under control and working for her, not against her. She thought she had complete freedom—but that was because she didn't have a budget or the experience to know what to plan for. Now she has a budget, an emergency fund, investments, *and* an allowance that she can spend on the things that she wants. It may not be as much as it was before, but she knows that all her major bases are covered and she has the *freedom* to spend in each category of her budget without fear of not having money to cover the necessary future expenses. It's not a blind freedom—it's a well calculated freedom. A well educated freedom. A knowing freedom. A freedom that allows her to take care of my grandson... and start her own business.

It's like living in a *free* country. Being in a free country does not mean that it doesn't *cost* you something. There is a cost for freedom. A great cost for freedom. Not only in terms of past and present lost life that many paid to secure this freedom, but in the ongoing vigilance that we all must have daily to ensure our life, liberty and pursuit of happiness. We owe an enormous debt to those who have paid the price to secure our *freedom*. I knew two young men personally who *gave it all* that you and I might have the freedoms this country offers. Plus, there are 848,000 more whom I don't know who have died in combat[40] and have paid the price of freedom over the two plus centuries of our existence (this doesn't include the non-combat dead or the wounded).

That's very humbling.

If we trivialize the cost of freedom, we will suffer the fate of every other nation that has fallen, and just like Stephanie wasn't prepared to pay the debt, we will not be prepared to ensure our freedom. But when we plan and prepare, just like Stephanie is now prepared to keep your heart pumping until she hands you off to the orderlies in the emergency room, and just like she is prepared financially for many different scenarios, we have a much better chance of survival—whether we're talking triage, finances, or our country's freedom. Freedom does *not* come from *not* knowing (ignorance is bliss only for a short time), freedom comes from being well informed, having adequate planning, and working hard at the plan.

So freedom does not mean ignorance. Freedom is well informed. You can't make good decisions without good input. At least not continuously sustainable.

So why are people afraid that if they make themselves accountable, they will lose their freedom? Because any time you give someone else the right to hold you accountable, you give up a little freedom. Not a lot, but a little—and of your own making. But remember—you're giving up the *bad* freedom to gain a *better* freedom.

Let's look at an analogy of wanting to save money to buy a car. You need a car for school next year, but don't have enough cash to buy one so you need to go to work this summer to save enough money to buy a used car for school. You were going to spend much of the summer at the beach, or the mountains, pool, playing Call of Duty...something *other* than working...

But, realizing you need to get ahead instead of playing your life away, you need to make some money to buy that car. So you trade in some of your freedom—summer fun—for cash—working for your neighbor. Not all your fun, but some of it. You have officially traded some of your freedom for another purpose.

However, at the moment, you're having so much fun at the beach, you can't get motivated to go to work. But you know it's the right thing to do. So you ask your buddy Mark to hold you accountable to get that job and start working by next Monday. Now Mark is part of your freedom system because accountability is part of that freedom system. But the bottom line is that, although accountability now (working for his neighbor) means freedom later (pay for car), it means you are trading some freedom now for more freedom later.

So it *feels* like you are losing freedom now. And, you are. But the value of the freedom you are trading for is a much greater value then the freedom you are giving up—otherwise it wouldn't be worth it. But the car means school, learning, graduation, diploma, job, career, advancement, family, home, yada, yada, yada.[41] Whatever your definition of success is. The time you may have spent at the beach will be a distant memory when you are making new memories with your life.

We are willing to trade small freedoms for larger ones. Rarely do we trade large freedoms for small ones, albeit it occasionally happens when we've had enough of the rat race, or enough pain, and we need a different kind of freedom. But that's the subject of many a contemporary psychology book and not this one...

So what am I saying? Don't look at Positive Accountability, or any accountability, as something that takes *away* your freedom. It's a freedom giver, not a freedom taker. In every case, you will trade a small freedom—i.e. trading an hour per day for good physical fitness/health, or trading $2,000 per year for 10 years (total of $20,000), for $1.2 million in compounding investments in 45 years (retirement funds), or any other situation where you trade one freedom—to gain a better freedom.

Whatever you want to accomplish, trading a little accountability for the freedom of whatever it is you seek is huge. Look on accountability as a freedom maker. It will help you get to where you want to go. At least for the 80% of us that are not self-finishers. Then, hopefully, one day we will become self-starters—and we'll still be trading lesser freedoms for greater ones.

Reflection and Practice—

• Everybody hates being told what to do, but kindly reminding people that want to be reminded is great..

• We trade one freedom for another.

• Saying *yes* to one thing is saying *no* to another. Simple logic. You can't have it all or do it all. It's the *Law of Sacrifice* (John Maxwell).

• Positive Accountability is a freedom giver—not a freedom taker.

Conclusion—

Don't look at Positive Accountability as something that takes away your freedom—look at it as something that gives you more freedom by helping you achieve your ultimate goals—because it *does* give you freedom and it *does* help you achieve.

—∿—

— 7 —

Staying on Target

"Nobody's a natural. You work to get good and then work to get better. It's hard to stay on top."
— Paul Gallico —

Gold Five: "Stabilize your rear deflectors... Watch for enemy fighters."
Gold Leader: "They're coming in! Three marks at 2-10! It's no good, I can't maneuver!"
Gold Five: "Stay on target."
Gold Leader: We're too close!"
Gold Five: "Stay on target!"
Gold Leader: "Loosen up!"
"BOOOOOM!"

Stay on target. Stay on target. That may have been the biggest mantra in our family from *Star Wars*—though, in reality, we probably cited 30-40 quotes often. Whenever anyone would waver in anything, out came "Stay on target!"

Unfortunately, the Star Wars reference didn't turn out well for Gold Leader. He was dispatched by the nefarious Darth Vader (I finally found a place in this book where I could use the word nefarious!).

I wonder why we used the quote so often when the reference was "when you stay on target you get blown up." Nonetheless, it was given as encouragement to see it through to completion. Keep doing the do until it's done!

So what does staying on target have to do with Positive Accountability? Remember building a habit that we discussed earlier? Well, you've got to stay on target that long in order to make it a habit. I want to give you some things to help you do that.

Wait. *Isn't the whole point of Positive Accountability to have an accountability partner to help me stay on target?* Yes. And eventually, hopefully, at least not most of the time, no. Your partner is not there to cajole, push, nag, whack, force, manipulate, bludgeon, ... They are there to *remind*. But that doesn't mean you will always do what you're reminded to do (imagine that...).

A great friend of mine joined a men's accountability group to be held accountable in his marriage. As it turned out, because he is such a good leader, several of the men, who had been sharing about their addiction to porn, came to him to ask him to hold them accountable in the area of pornography—it's *not* an area he suffers in.

This next part is bizarre. There is software[42] that you can put on your computer that will email or text someone if you start watching porn. Yep. That's what I said. So their accountability partner can text or call them and say "RUN!" from the porn. These guys were serious about beating their addiction and enlisted my friend and this technology to battle this debilitating scourge.

Now, Positive Accountability partnerships aren't this aggressive. But drastic situations require drastic measures, and this tactic was appropriate for the situation.

In this case, as well as with Positive Accountability, we can decide *not* to do what we should be doing—what our partner is reminding us about. That's what freedom is all about. But the desire, and the point, is to stay on target and *not* fail—with or *without* our partner.

How do we ensure we are working the problem and not *only* relying on the efforts of our accountability partner to keep us going? Many ways.

I love the quote at the beginning of this chapter. "Nobody's a natural. You work to get good and then work to get better. It's hard to stay on top." It *is* hard to stay on top. Nobody is born perfect or the best at something. Some of us have greater gifts in certain areas, but it really does take a lot of work to be good at something and a lot more to be great at it. Take the *"5 Levels of Leadership"* test by John Maxwell, and you'll discover some tough things about yourself. Most people don't score as well as they think they will. And that's okay—as long as you're willing to learn and grow. You can download the test for IOS *only* here—

www.roycewhite.com/jm-5-levels-test/

As you tackle each of the items on your list that you want to be held accountable to accomplish, you need to do some homework to set up your offense and defense to help you get there. Self-finishers see the target—the goal—and push themselves to completion. So let's borrow from them to stay on target.

I have identified 7 things that you can do to help you stay on target. The more you put into place, the more you are likely to finish.

1. Photos. Find a photo of your goal and put it on your morning bathroom mirror so you see it first thing in the morning and last thing at night. When he decided to lose weight, motivational speaker, Zig Ziglar put a photo of a skinny man torn from a jockey underwear advertisement on his mirror. First thing every morning and last thing at night he would see his goal—to be skinny—staring him in the face. John Maxwell learned a sense of urgency from W. Clement Stone, who told his audience, "Before you get out of bed every morning, say 'do it now' fifty times." [43]

Whatever it takes to get you on track each day, put a picture of that in your face. With so many smartphone/cameras, you can make your own picture and put it up there. I have this love/hate thing with torn pages from a magazine; on the one hand, it makes it difficult for me to read, but on the other, I know somebody, somewhere, sometime, is getting more done.

Also, put this same photo above your computer at work, on your refrigerator, on your car dashboard, etc. The point is to remind yourself often—at least until you build a habit.

2. Quotes. Search the web for "quotes about..."

- being assertive
- accomplishment
- motivation
- inspiration
- getting things done
- accountability
- enthusiasm
- optimism
- courage
- time management
- and any you can think of that are positive reinforcements.

Copy the quotes that resonate with you on to a card and put them on your fridge, on your car dash, on your wallet, screen saver—anywhere you will see them often. This will take you 15 to 20 minutes to set up but will work for you the rest of your life reminding you of the attitude you need to meet your goal. Memorize these!!

3. Eliminate things that go against your goal. When you're on diet, you get the things out of the house that you tend to eat that are not on your diet. Do this with *everything* that is not pushing you toward your goal. Move the temptation—better yet, flee from it! Trash it—get it away. Same with things that will stop you from reaching your goal. Eliminate them. Stop spending time online shopping if spending money is the issue. You get the idea. You've got to give up to go up. Give up the things that slow you from achievement. Make a list of these things and annihilate them! BOOM!

4. Full Organization. Schedule every moment. One of the top things you can do *in life* to stay on target (and just in general), keep out of trouble and accomplish your goal, is to schedule your *complete* day. Schedule everything and I mean everything (well, almost).

Below is one day of my scheduling program. From when I wake at 4:29a, to when I go to bed at 10:30p, everything is scheduled—even free-time—in half-hour increments. If you schedule all your time, there will be less opportunity to get sidetracked, plus you have the added benefit of accomplishing a lot of things. You can put your

A day in the life of Royce...

own reminders in there for your own accountability. It takes me 10-15 minutes maximum per day to keep this, and sometimes only five minutes. I set it up a week in advance and tweak it as necessary and specifically the night before. Studies have shown that 15 minutes a day planning can save up to two hours per day in wasted time.[44] That's 730 hours per year. That's 5 *years* over your lifetime. (What's in your wallet!) What can you do with 5 years? Heck, give it to me if you don't want it.

Get your hands on a Franklin Planner, a DayTimer, Scheduler App for your Smartphone, or something that works for you (operative word is "works for *you*"). I don't care if you're a student, a salesperson, a homemaker, or a rocket scientist. Time is the most precious thing we have; and, if you use it well, you will always be satisfied with your day. If you waste it, you will end up like the 4,000 executives of Dr. Bell who wished they had taken charge of their lives sooner (scheduled their lives better) and set goals earlier. BTW, you can't get my app above. I created it myself years ago and it automates a lot of things so although it's a great tool for me, you'll have to rely on one of the other tools out there, and there are good ones. See the Appendix for a list of top paper planners and Planner Apps.[45]

5. Carry a token as a reminder. Over the years, I have carried a number of items in a pocket every day to remind me of something I want to think about often. This includes a special key, a token on leadership, a cross, a AA battery, a lock nut, a nail, and more. Each one had a specific significance that I understood and reminded me about something each time I happened to put my hand in my pocket. It's very effective and helps me stay on target a little bit at a time. I saw this one on the internet... maybe we'll get some challenge coins and offer them.

6. Establish Milestones and celebrate small wins. Be *immediate* and *specific*. If you are specific about your goal (lose 30 pounds by December 31st; write a book in 365 days one page per day; get out of debt by November 16th; get my degree by May 31st; sell my car and move to Venezuela...), you can create milestones and celebrate along the way. It is *always* good to set milestones (and it's definitely great to celebrate!). This way you know whether or not you are on target and if you need to pick up on your action items to complete the goal on time. For instance, if you are losing 30 pounds over 6 months, that's 5 pounds per month, or roughly 1.190476 pounds per week. Roughly...

At the end of each month, you can have a celebration if you are on target. I usually recommend celebrating with something outside of your goal area (meaning, don't have a piece of chocolate cake to celebrate losing 5 pounds). Movie night out, layaway at your favorite store some new clothes at your final weight, some treat that is a simple, nice reward. Things that will help you celebrate but keep going. Does this make sense?

7. Get your thinkin' cap on straight. Time to get "stinkin thinkin" out of your head. Many times over the course of your accountability on the way to your goal, you will encounter "stinkin thinkin"— thoughts that pull you down and take you off target. (I believe it was Zig Ziglar who coined the 'stinkin thinkin' phrase.) While [#]2 above on Quotes is a good reminder for the day, you can fill your mind with a lot more ideas and quotes—not just the couple you print out and post around your life. When the going gets tough, you will need as much positive thinking as possible to help keep you on target. Here are 11 great thinkin' quotes. To read hundreds more, go to

roycewhite.com/all-quotes/

Memorize these! Get them pulsing through your veins and your brain.

1. People often say that motivation doesn't last. Well, neither does bathing. That's why we recommend it daily. —Zig Ziglar

2. I am not a product of my circumstances. I am a product of my decisions. —Stephen Covey

3. Either you run the day, or the day runs you. —Jim Rohn

4. Ask and it will be given to you; search, and you will find; knock and the door will be opened for you. —Jesus

5. When I stand before God at the end of my life, I would hope that I would not have a single bit of talent left and could say, I used everything you gave me. —Erma Bombeck

6. Certain things catch your eye, but pursue only those that capture the heart. —Ancient Indian Proverb

7. Too many of us are not living our dreams because we are living our fears. —Les Brown

8. I have been impressed with the urgency of doing. Knowing is not enough; we must apply. Being willing is not enough; we must do. —Leonardo da Vinci

9. The person who says it cannot be done should not interrupt the person who is doing it. —Chinese Proverb

10. I have learned over the years that when one's mind is made up, this diminishes fear. —Rosa Parks

11. When everything seems to be going against you, remember that the airplane takes off against the wind, not with it. —Henry Ford

It's awesome to have great inspirational quotes flying around all day but we *also* need to get doubt and fear forced out of our heads. It's like the Lamaze method of child birth. Part of it is concentrating on an object to make it tougher for the pain to control our thought process during contractions. Our conscious minds don't do well thinking about two things at once (except for when we put things into muscle memory and they work from our subconscious). If we flood our minds with good and positive things, there is less time and space for the negative stuff.

Dwell on realizing your goal. See yourself at the end of your goal having obtained it, owning it. If you say yes to one thing, you're saying no to the other. Fill your mind with all the good stuff you can and force out that nasty, nefarious, yucky stuff.

Reflection and Practice—

• Building habits is one of the keys to reaching your goal. Do what you gotta do to stay on target.

• Post photos of your end goal around your office, home, computer.

• Hang a couple of key quotes (or even just your goal) around the places you work and live to act as constant reminders.

• Eliminate anything that goes against your goal. (keep kids, though)

• Get Organized! Plan out your success!

• Carry a Token or a lapel pin around to remind you every time you stick your hand in your pocket or look in the mirror.

• Establish milestones and celebrate small wins.

• Work to beat stinkin thinkin.

Conclusion—

There are any number of things you can do. Do as many as you need to in order to succeed. Don't be limited by my suggestions. Do the Homework and get your own, and accomplish.

"I attribute my success to this: I never gave or took any excuse. "
—Florence Nightingale

— 8 —

Pay or Play?

"You can never cross the ocean until you have the courage to lose sight of the shore."
— Christopher Columbus —

One of my biggest desires in life is to help people accomplish. Whatever they want. Anything. To get from where they are to where they want to be, as long as it is isn't illegal, immoral, or unethical.

I find that people have great ideas. Most people, if not all, have a good-to-great idea every day. Leo Widrich, a blogger from Buffer, cited several fMRI studies on brain activity during creativity and subsequently noted, "The truth, which I was very happy to discover, is that any and everybody is creative. In fact, we are all extremely creative." [46] *The key is to get the ideas recorded as quickly as possible.*

It's like a dream. Within five minutes of waking from a dream, 50% of the dream is forgotten. After 10 minutes, 90% is gone. [47] For me, an idea can fly out of my head as fast as it came in—sometimes in mere seconds. Sometimes it's gone before I finish the creative thought!

I believe it was the mega entrepreneur, Richard Branson, who said that sometimes he forgets ideas as fast as he thinks of them. Well, at least the billionaire with over 300 companies and I have something in common—I forget ideas as fast as I have them as well. Now if I could just figure out how to share in some of his other traits... :)

One of Richard's mantras is that you have to take the necessary risks in order to accomplish. Many people don't like risk. But without it, you'll never launch the ship to get to the new land (see Columbus quote last page). You'll stay in your comfort zone on the dry land.

The biggest problem, as I have addressed it elsewhere, is "getting started." Once you do get going, the key is to stay in the game long enough to get a "path" built in your brain—a *habit*—muscle/brain memory. Not that you will be great at something as you are forming a habit, but you have made the *process* a habit. If the process is a habit, it's just a matter of staying on target to conclusion. What does it take to help you stay in the game? One of the greatest ways to be committed is to have *skin in the game.*

For a definition, to have "skin in the game" is to have incurred monetary risk by being invested in achieving a goal.[48] So the idea is that if you want to stay on target, you should have some skin in the game to help keep you on target. The *Omaha Oracle*—and second richest man in America (2014)—Warren Buffet, is credited with coining the phrase *skin in the game* as it relates to high-ranking insiders using their personal money to buy stock in the company *they* are running. This will ensure that companies are managed by individuals who share a stake in the company's success—and failure.

As a professional coach, I have full paying clients and a few free clients (family, friends, etc.), as well as some potential skeptical clients to whom I offer one or two free sessions. In general they are unfamiliar with coaching or have had a bad experience from a bad coach, and, hence, don't believe coaching works (although they are quickly won over).

Because they have skin in the game, my full-paying clients don't fool around. They get straight to the point, and, during the sessions, work very hard at getting to the solutions. On the other hand, because there is no cost (no *skin in the game*), my free clients do not take it as seriously. There are countless stories in my life as well as your own life that point to the truth of this concept. My dad proved it over and over again in my life when making me work for something and thereby, making the "thing" more valuable to me.

Another example. My bride Jody and I teach *Lindy Hop* swing dancing. It's a great exercise (lost 35 pounds), keeps me in shape, and gives us something to do together that we both like. We've taught thousands of people over the past 16 years. We also do private parties, receptions, etc.—usually a 45-minute lesson and then I DJ the dance.

Whenever we do a *private* party, the lesson and dance is a secondary element—meaning the Christmas party, etc., is the primary element. Although the event planners pay us to do the event, the attendees don't pay for it. After we get there, set up, and are ready to go, we announce what we are going to do—lesson and dance—and *strongly* invite people up to participate. We usually get about a third to one half of the crowd to come up and dance with us. All those who participate have a good time, and, after the lesson, those that did *not* join in the lesson share a regret that they did not get involved—usually because it *looked like fun*. And it is fun—a lot of fun. Too much fun.

The people that did *not* participate didn't take the risk and didn't get the reward. They had no skin in the game, so they didn't reap the benefit. If you take some time to reflect, I'm sure you will see there are many events in your own life where this rings true. We usually just shrug it off and never visit it again.

Hence, getting some skin in the game helps us get to accomplishment better and gives us reason to stay on target when the going gets tougher. At the very least, it's better than NOT having skin in the game—just like having a positive attitude may not necessarily make you better, but it is better than having a bad attitude every time!

So how do you get *your* skin in the game of Positive Accountability?

1. *Rewards*. If you really want something, raise one of your goals and tag the item on as a reward. For instance, I have a specific goal for this book. If I sell the number of copies I have in my goal, I will buy a Seadoo Personal Watercraft as a "reward"—that is, if I can talk my bride into it... :-). Gives me a lot more incentive to help move the book. Granted, I could just go buy the Seadoo, but this gives me some competition with myself and gives me a reward if I do it.

I do this for smaller, everyday wins, too. I have a pretty good diet. Partially because my bride needs to eat well because of some health issues, partly because my daughter is my trainer and is fearless and ruthless, and partly because I *want* to have good health. Once every couple of weeks I get to have some chocolate. So when I know I am going to have it, I pick a chore to do, or a task I want to accomplish and tell myself I can have the chocolate when I am done with it. I reward myself *and* accomplish a task I have been putting off. Yes, I could have eaten the chocolate anyway, but I have built this (and am still building it) to help me accomplish more.

You can do it with other things, too. For example (and *only* example)—

• Finish a project and reward yourself by doing something you love.
• Finish the school year with a 3.5 average and go to the closest theme park for the day or weekend.
• Hit your weight goal and buy some new clothes or other treat.
• Hit your sales goals and take a special vacation.
• Be on time for a month (for those with trouble being on time) and reward yourself with something.

Why do the rewards always have to come from others? Setup your own system or rewards.

You can do this with a lot of things. It brings it to light and gives you something to strive/work for. For me, I recently discovered I need more rewards—or at least more things to look forward to. I don't plan vacations. I grew up not going on many vacations and got into the bad habit of not taking enough vacations with my own family (apology to my bride and kids—we should have done a lot more. Please forgive me...). I would travel a lot for work, trade shows, sales meetings, competition to report on, worldwide reps to visit, etc., and sometimes

I would take the family. That sounds gallant for work, and is definitely better than nothing, but it really is a cop-out. Yea, I've heard all the stories of how great it was from lots of folks that did it. Hogwash. Vacation time needs to be sacrosanct. With 20/20 hindsight, I would do it quite differently, separating out business and pleasure. I would have learned to relax and recoup far better and it would have had a much better effect upon my family—and isn't it the betterment of my family that I'm working for in the first place?

So now, I specifically plan vacations four times a year. It gives me something to look forward to every three months, and I discovered I really, really, really need to have these times to look forward to—even though I absolutely love what I do.

I go visit my mom and dad in Florida in February (the week after a John Maxwell event), take a week off with my bride around our anniversary in June, take a week off and go to the beach in September with some great, longtime friends, and take off a couple of weeks at Christmas time when family and friends come in (we have five children and as of this writing two grandchildren, but I am sure more will be on the way in the future! (no pressure kids...)).

So rewarding yourself is a great thing to do and a way to put more *skin in the game*. If I don't sell the books, I don't get the Watercraft... I'll have to settle for a kayak.... but I love kayaking, too!

2. *Challenge. Competition. Contest.* Find someone to compete with. Even if it's not an official competition. Many of us are competitive—some very competitive. Some people say competition is bad, citing

things more related to comparison than competition. We compare ourselves and our traits, attribute, etc., with others. Yes, this is destructive. With competition, I am talking about a race, a challenge, a friendly wager.

I see a friend online losing a lot of weight when I'm on diet, too. I have a goal and so do they. So I challenge them to reach the goal first. Or I may even just challenge them in my mind and use them as a goal without telling them. There are many ways to be competitive in a positive way.

I remember a business colleague of mine back in the 1990s. I was buying his product and bundling it with my product. One day in our normal conversation, we realized we had started our businesses almost at the same time—at least the same year, and, if I recall correctly, just a month or two apart. We were in about our fifth year, both businesses doing well, with a bright future for each of us. The major difference was that whether his business did well or poorly, it would have little effect on my business, but if my business did well, it would certainly help his business because we were selling his software with our hardware. To be sure, a major difference.

I wanted to do well for both our sakes. We talked about where we were going with each of our companies and he looked like he had a great future. At some point I said to him, "Let's check back in 10 years and see who has gone the farthest." He laughed and we promised to touch base. I can tell you without hesitation, he won the offhand *wager*. In three years, he had sold his company to a huge company for 55 million dollars, bought a villa in Italy, and was selling high-end olive oil. I was still struggling to survive.

Did either of us run our businesses differently because of the wager? I doubt it. I know I didn't and I'm fairly certain he didn't either. We were already pushing the companies for a far better reason than a friendly wager. We were already succeeding and looking to succeed more in the future. We didn't need the accountability.

Competition only works when the goal is a small goal, with a much shorter time line than three years. Or, if we were both competing in the same field, competition might give us impetus to accomplish more. We were both already driven and pushing toward success. We didn't need accountability to move toward success. We knew what we wanted, knew how to get there, and we were using all that we had to accomplish it. We needed another kind of accountability, but not one to get or stay on target.

3. *Pay to play*—hire a coach. As I said in Chapter 1, and will reiterate throughout the book, although having accountability is a part of coaching, coaching is *far* more than accountability. A coach will dig deep by asking you curiosity based questions that you will not think of yourself, that will get you to search your subconscious to find the solutions and answers you seek in order to bring out the direction you should go. If you do not succeed with just Positive Accountability, which will be all that is needed for many situations and topics, then you should take a good look at using a coach. And for this professional service you should be *willing* to pay. If you get the right coach, it is sooooo worth it.

Good coaches, like those trained and certified by the John Maxwell Team, are trained to help you get to where you really want to go. They have honed and practiced their skills to a point where they can adeptly draw out your experience, wisdom, and ability, in order to help you achieve your highest goals.

As certified professional coaches, we are not mentoring—though we are excellent mentors and sometimes we will use mentoring to help. We are not counselors—though we sometimes refer you to one. We are not friends, though much of the time we may know you better than a friend. We are not consultants, though many of us would make good consultants. We are coaches and leaders, whose main goal is to listen so intently between the lines to help you achieve long term goals and short term outcomes, to significantly understand and reflect back what the reality of what you think is so you can discover hidden thoughts and ideas, to explore options, and to help uncover the best way forward. There are three wonderful things for a coach to hear a client say during a coaching session—

1. *"That's a great question."* Realization that this question—one you haven't asked yourself before—will lead to a new answer.

2. *"Did I say that?"* Realization that you're not reflecting on your own thoughts enough (listening deeply enough).

and finally,

3. " "
Silence. Indicating some deep, deep, deep introspection.

Coaching is definitely one of the best tools you can use to get unstuck, determine direction, and get to your goal much more quickly. It is the best money you can spend to get to your goal. I have been both client and coach. I have been coached to some great changes in my life—some very tough decisions that I was not coming to on my own. As well, I have coached and do coach others to some great successes. I love what it does for people.

Based upon my research on the web which includes several studies, in today's (2014) dollars, the average life coach charges $200 per hour and the average executive coach charges $500 plus per hour. More specialized coaches or ones for sales, CEOs, or fast-growing larger companies can charge several times that amount. That sounds like a lot of money until you weigh that against getting to the end of your life and realizing you didn't fulfill your dreams or desires. Then, it's a very small price to pay to move forward. It really is.

A coach can bring you to a solution in just one session, or it can take several months depending upon the desired outcome. What I find in my practice is that it takes a couple to a few sessions to deal with the issue; and, then because it worked so well and so fast, the client wants to gain control and success in other areas of her life or business and keeps coming back for more sessions. The average time I work with clients in coaching is about nine months—and we have usually covered quite a number of topics. I have never had a client say that it wasn't worth *far* more than the cost. The cost is only one time—the solutions last for a lifetime.

The simple bottom line is, it will cost you more if you don't use a coach—guaranteed. The cost of *not* achieving your goal is far greater then the cost of hiring a coach. The time and money you waste because of the natural human tendencies we have, or, more importantly, the things you don't accomplish because of not hiring a coach, can all be avoided, and you can be on your way to getting on with your life, growing your business, and realizing your life goals far sooner than later.

My apologies if you've ever had a bad coach. Like anything, there are some bad ones out there—and because there is no official governing body of coaches, you can get someone who sounds good, but does not have the skill necessary to help you the best. So many people call themselves coaches today and are really consultants or mentors and do not understand the true methodology and procedure of being a coach. Coaches are not typically experts in your industry—and that's good! You almost *don't* want a coach who understands your specific line of work—it makes it too easy for the coach to fall into mentoring or consulting instead of true coaching. Coaches understand... the *process*.

The relationship between client and coach. THAT'S what gets to the core—that's what gets the job done. We know how to draw out the answers that are deep inside of you—answers that you cannot get to without good coaching. You see, YOU know your business and your industry far better than we do and we know coaching far better than you do. We bring the two together to find the correct answer for your desired outcome. It is, truly, a symbiotic relationship—and it works.

You *can* find a good coach. Because this list is always growing and changing, I have a listing on my website of certified professional coaches, of whom I personally know the quality of their coaching. I list them here so you don't have to worry about finding one who knows what they are doing. These coaches are certified and *hand picked* by me for this purpose. I want you to get the best out there. More importantly, coaches that will help you get to where you really, really, really want to go.

Go to this link and choose the one closest to you, the one with the coolest sounding name, or the one with the most interesting resume. It doesn't really matter. They are *all* very, very good and will help you quickly get the solutions you desire.

roycewhite.com/coaches/

Also in the Appendix in the back of this book.

I'm not pushing coaches if all you need is accountability—just the opposite. I'm pushing Positive Accountability methodology—but if you're stuck or Positive Accountability isn't working, you now have somewhere you can go for help to get your life going.

In one way or another, it will cost you. In lost opportunity, or ensuring success, you need to have skin in the game, realize the cost, and pursue it. Anything in life that is worth working for is worth paying for. There are many ways to pay. I've given you some options in this chapter. Choose which way you can afford and attack it! You may have to invest time, money, energy—or all the above. Decide what is worth it to you and jump. Today. Now. Are you still here?

Reflection and Practice—

• Take the necessary risks in order to accomplish.

• Stay in the game long enough to get a "path" built in your brain—a *habit*—muscle/brain memory—anywhere from 30 to 200 days! Depends upon who you are.

• You have to have *skin in the game,* a cost to you, to help you stay on target.

• You need rewards to give yourself something to look forward to—even beyond the goal itself.

• Get some friendly competition going to help you keep your sight on the end.

• When the goal is *really* big, get some paid coaching; it will pay for itself almost from the very beginning and help you achieve your goal.

• Get out of your comfort zone and into your capacity zone!

• Remember—*"Positive thinking will let you do everything better than negative thinking will."* —Zig Ziglar

—ɯɯ—

— 9 —

The Accountability Partnerships

**"Perfect partners don't exist. Perfect conditions exist
for a limited time in which partnerships
express themselves best."**
— Wayne Rooney —

I realize that not everyone has a partner available to them at the drop of
a hat. Finding the perfect partner, as Wayne says above, isn't easy. You
may know the perfect person and away you go. You're done. Thanks
for reading. It's been a pleasure. Go conquer all your heart's delight!

Or, you may not know anybody that you can go to yet. So we decided
to create a database of people that want to find and have accountability
partners as soon as possible. Boom.

We have created *The Accountability Partnerships* website. It's part
of our regular website. There you will find a place for you to enter
your own information—all totally confidential. We don't even look at
it. The program behind it all blindly looks at the data. Everybody else
who has joined the Partnership has answered the same questions.

We have labored long and hard to create an algorithm that will put you together with someone who we believe you will share a good accountability partnership with. The system may be wrong, but you're never stuck. If it's not working for you, you can sign in to your account and ask for and get a new partner.

Every person must read and sign our confidentiality agreement and must agree to abide by the rules, which are not extensive, but are important. There are methods and procedures to follow to get the best experience from the partnerships—not to mention the best success from it. The confidentiality agreement is on line when you sign up.

Let me make sure I am clear about what this is. You are both partners to one another. There are two partners in each partnership. Partner A will hold Partner B accountable for his/her goal and Partner B will hold Partner A accountable for his/her goal. This is a two-way accountability because we are pulling from a list of people that all want to be involved. There is no sense in the two people in a partnership holding other people accountable.

So the following scenario will *not* happen—Partner A holds Partner B accountable and Partner B holds Partner C accountable and Partner C holds Partner A accountable, etc.

If you are really motivated, you could have two different partners holding you accountable for different things (or, come to think of it, you could have *both* of them holding you accountable for the same thing if you really wanted a lot of input, but that's a little severe...).

Hence, this is a two-way partnership. You may do all your accountability at the same time or at different times. That will be totally up to you. Here are the basic rules for ensuring a great experience with partnerships—whether using your partner or one from our website.

Partnership Rules—

1. Honor the other partner's time by contacting at the agreed upon times. Don't call or text randomly—the partner's work/life schedule may find him asleep when you are making noise on his smartphone. Agree to the time and follow it.

2. Don't use this Partnership for anything else. This is strictly for holding one another accountable—not for building friends, though you may become friends, not for coaching, consulting, or counseling. It really is best this way.

3. Rude, crude, and socially unacceptable—*Don't be*. Don't assume your partner is just like you in all ways. Don't use bad language, don't be mean, nagging, angry, unkind, etc.

4. *Do* keep everything positive and uplifting. Be thoughtful and selfless (not selfish).

5. Don't teach your partner—you're not here to give advice. Even if you have good advice. If you want to begin a mentorship, you can do so outside of the accountability program. That's your business.

6. Do not be fraudulent in any way. Do not ask for or give money to a partner. Do not lie—have the courage and character to say, "I didn't do it" or "I don't know."

7. Do not offer anything for sale to your partner. This is not an avenue for increasing your sales. This is for helping one another achieve your goals.

8. Be faithful to execute your part of the partnership in a timely fashion.

9. Be responsible and be accountable! Do your topic!

10. Work hard at achieving your goal. Don't sign up for this only to ignore or not work at it.

This isn't exhaustive—just some common principles that will help you stay on target with your partner.

This will be an exciting time as you work toward reaching your goal, and slowly—or quickly—achieving it. In general, slow and steady wins this race. If you're willing to do the homework, you will achieve the success you are looking for. If you're not willing, you shouldn't look forward to success. It will continually elude you until you are willing to make the investment. It's always worked that way, and always will. But it's not hard—this is one of the best ways I know to start achieving when you're not a great self-starter.

To begin your partnership, go to this link below and fill out the form. There is a minimal monthly charge for our administration and to ensure you have some *skin in the game* (see Chapter 8, Pay or Play?).

This is an awesome opportunity to get started right away and be on your way to success with your goal.. or many goals. I am part of the system because I want to be hands on so I can constantly make it better, so you may have me as a partner from time to time!

Looking forward to seeing you there.

roycewhite.com/accountability-partnerships

— 10 —

Conclusion/Epilogue

"Let others lead small lives, but not you. Let others argue over small things, but not you. Let others cry over small hurts, but not you. Let others leave their future in someone else's hands, but not you."
— Jim Rohn —

Bottom line: You want to succeed at your goal. You want to accomplish. It's that simple. The problems are many fold as we have discovered, the biggest one being that we are part of the 80% who *are* not or *have not* become self-starters. We've dealt with a bunch of objections throughout this book. You may still have your own. But the truth is, it's up to you to make this happen. Positive Accountability is here to help you get started and grow along the way.

The whole point of finding and working with an accountability partner is to build habits and help defeat the struggle to stay on target. This accountability methodology will help you during this tough period—use it. I outlined in chapter 5 exactly how to do this, and included a form to help you set it up. We also talked about things *you* can do to help *you* succeed.

Let's recap.

In **Chapter 1**, we defined what Positive Accountability is—working with another person as your partner to remind you of your commitment, based upon an agreed upon schedule. With accountability partners, as in the Jenny Craig study, we should have a high level of success (they had 92%).

We discussed that we need to build habits, and we need to build them into brain/muscle memory to make it a habit.

We also talked a little about the differences between Positive Accountability and professional coaching and about which methodology is the best to use at what time.

We introduced the idea that the toughest part of getting started, is getting started. JUMP! Get started!

Conclusion, it takes two to conquer your goal when you don't have the tenacity or *startability* to do it on your own. It's okay to get someone to help you. Better to get someone to help and then accomplish your goal than to do it on your own and never get started. Be willing and reach out to someone to help you accomplish this.

Chapter 2 was about defining success. We talked about success being something that is individually oriented. No one else can define success for you. You must take the time to define it, or you won't hit it.

We talked about success being like a blindfolded archer who can't hit his target—if you can't see your target, you can't hit it. Further, you don't even know which way to shoot.

Defining success and goals gives you the clarity you need in life to take your best shot.

We talked about asking yourself a lot of questions and being curious about your hopes and dreams. Where do they all point?

We talked about the 7 Streams of Life and how knowing where you are in them and what you want to achieve in them will help you define success.

Conclusion: Knowing *your* definition of success is critical because without it, you cannot really know the depth of the direction you want for accountability. Take some time and define it and write it down!

Chapter 3 was about being a self-starter / self-finisher and that only about 20% of us are true self-starters.

We talked about getting help to get and stay focused. I told the story of a past business and of putting up the Christmas lights.

We talked about the tenacity to stay on target and that it is *sometimes* harder than self-starting.

Conclusion: get help before you get into trouble. Get it when you start.

Chapter 4 is about balance. We talked about the need to be balanced or the unbalanced areas will slow you or stop you from succeeding in the area in which you want to grow.

We discussed that the proper balance will help you make sure you are spending the right time on the right things.

We talked about Dr. Gerald Bell and the 4,000 retired executives study.

Being well balanced allows you to put your priorities in place and concentrate on the greatest area of weakness.

We discussed the Wheel of Life and how to use it to be better balanced.

Conclusion: You must have good balance or be heading positively in that direction so you're not thwarted in your shot at your goal.

Chapter 5 we discussed exactly how to set up a Positive Accountability partnership complete with forms and a definition of each item.

We said to choose your topic, give it the reasonability test, write the goal down in a complete, readable, cohesive paragraph—preferably in your own handwriting—make a poster, card, sign, and find a partner.

We defined what this partner "looks" like in personality, etc., and we talked about exactly how it works.

Conclusion: Use these tools and definitions to help find your perfect—or not so perfect—accountability partner.

Chapter 6 on accountability and freedom. We talked about freedom and how it affects accountability.

We discussed trading one freedom for another; saying yes to one thing is saying no to another.

Positive Accountability is a freedom giver not a freedom taker.

Conclusion: Don't look at Positive Accountability as something that takes away your freedom—look at it as something that gives you more freedom by helping you achieve your ultimate goals.

Chapter 7, staying on target. We discussed many methods and helps that will keep you on top. Photos, quotes, eliminating things that go against your goal, full organization, carrying a token as a reminder, establishing milestones and celebrating small wins, and getting your thinking and attitude straight.

Chapter 8, pay or play.... we talked about the need to have *skin in the game*. We discussed three ways to get skin in the game—rewards, competition, and coaching.

Chapter 9 is about the *Positive Accountability, Accountability Partnerships* and how to be involved in that.

And this is **Chapter 10**—conclusions and epilogue.

I want to encourage you and challenge you. I work with people every week, almost every day, that once were stuck but now are succeeding. So I see good coaching work most of the time. Accountability is a portion of coaching and can be applied without having a coach. Granted, a good coach is well trained to work with you way beyond accountability, but there are plenty of things that do not require a coach and can be accomplished through Positive Accountability.

As we've discussed in this book, there are things you can do to move yourself toward success, and I've outlined how to do them according to the methodology and procedures of Positive Accountability. Whenever I hear someone say, "The easiest way to do this (any subject) is...". I like to jest with them by saying that the easiest way to do that is have someone else do it for you. Yes, I am joking, but there is some truth in it. Although we don't have our accountability partners do the work of what we want to accomplish, they do lend a hand in helping us get to it and do it—continuously!

Like the Jenny Craig study, I believe you have at least a 92% chance of succeeding at whatever you want to with Positive Accountability— although the caveat is that if the subject really needs in-depth coaching, you may only see marginal success. Some things—big things, huge things, deep things—require the skill and adroitness of a coach to help you gain the tools to self-finish. But again, having said that, it is well worth the effort to try Positive Accountability first before calling a coach—unless you already know it is going to require a coach.

Positive Accountability is not to be used to get around personal responsibility. It's here to help you get started, and then learn and experience that getting started and having tenacity will get you to your goal. Having a partner gives you a little extra help as you *learn* to be a self-starter and accomplish your goals.

I challenge you to get an accountability partner, fill out the form and test it—try it for something in which you have wanted success. Don't just read this book and say, "That was a nice book." Pick your topic—pick it right now and fill out the Positive Accountability form from Chapter 5 or from my website, and try it. I believe you will be surprised at how well it works. If you already have a ton of excuses why it won't work, then you may need a coach to call your bluff and help you directly. But if you know what you want to achieve and know how to get there and just need someone to keep you on target, you have everything to gain and success is closer than you think. It's like looking at the right outside mirror on your car—you know, the one that says, "Objects in mirror are closer than they appear."

If you don't think Positive Accountability can help you, test it out anyway. The investment is miniscule compared to the potential gain *and* well worth the effort. Can you imagine if we could get a portion of the 80% non self-starters becoming more successful? Canadian former professional ice hockey player Wayne Gretsky said, "You miss 100% of the shots you don't take."

In reviewing his career, a former NBA player once said, "I've missed more than 9,000 shots in my career. I've lost almost 300 games. 26 times, I've been trusted to take the game winning shot and *missed*. I've failed over and over and over again in my life. And that is why I succeed."

Have you lost over 300 times at your job? I dare say if I had a record like that in business, I would be out of business. But that is the nature of the NBA business. Not only has he lost over 300 games, but he is arguably the best player the NBA has ever seen. Moreover, he is the owner and chairman of the *Charlotte Hornets*. Who is this power-house? Michael Jordan. Yep. He has an estimated net worth over $650 million with an annual salary of $80 million.

Look what all that failure got him! A whole lot *more* success. Michael had a coach (sport). My guess is, he also had plenty of accountability.

You too can succeed at the goal you are shooting for. You're prob-ably not shooting for the $650 million, maybe you are, but whatever it is—it may be simple, like losing 35 pounds, learning to schedule, or increasing your sales, or maybe it's more complex like recording an album, selling your paintings, or starting a small business, or maybe it's something big like learning a language, doubling your sales, or going back to school for a degree after 20 years—whatever it is, you are fearfully and wonderfully made, you are part of a species that has gone to the moon, seen beyond the stars, mapped the ocean floor, built a mechanical heart, found exotic cures for many diseases, overcome gravity, harnessed electrons, housed billions, fed the hungry, helped the poor, created laughter, helped your neighbor—and if we can ac-complish those things together, we should be able to tackle anything else you can dream of.

Take no prisoners. Set your heart and mind toward reaching your goal, find your accountability partner, grab the Accountability Form on page 86, and begin!

In the immortal words of Zig Ziglar, "You don't have to be great to start, but you have to *start* to be great." It's time to start.

Dive in! There's a tidal wave coming—overtake it before it overtakes you!

Much love and blessing...

Your friend,
Royce

—⁓—

Thank you for taking the time to read this book. A piece of my heart and soul went into writing it. I hope that it gave you the impetus to try this methodology for yourself and move toward a better success. I would love to have your feedback as you work through Positive Accountability. Please contact me at the email below with your stories of success and hardship. I would love to hear your story of life and how you overcame to succeed. Or, if you have a question, ask me at this email or on my blog at RoyceWhite.com. Plus, I also get on the road speaking from time to time—I would love to see your face at an event. Blessings!

royce@roycewhite.com

Appendix

1. Links

Great links to great places for all sorts of related things.

My Website
www.roycewhite.com
Errata sheet for this book
http://www.roycewhite.com/pa-errata

John Maxwell's Website
http://www.johnmaxwell.com/

John Maxwell Five Levels of Leadership Test
http://www. roycewhite.com/jm-5-levels-test

Zig Ziglar's Website
http://www.ziglar.com

Les Brown's Website
http://lesbrown.com/

Brian Tracy's Website
http://www.briantracy.com

Good Quotes
http:www.roycewhite.com/all-quotes
http://www.brainyquote.com/

2. My favorite leadership, business, productivity book list.

This is a great list of books to help you grow and get to where you really, really, really want to go. This list is semi-sorted in a way that reflects my recommended reading order; meaning the order is helpful but not sacrosanct. I don't endorse every concept the authors put forth, neither will you, but there is typically more good than bad, and most of these—most—are very good and spot on. There is something you can glean from all of them.

The 15 Invaluable Laws of Growth, by John C. Maxwell
48 Days to the Work You Love, by Dan Miller
The 21 Irrefutable Laws of Leadership, by John C. Maxwell
Eat That Frog!, by Brian Tracy
Failing Forward, by John C. Maxwell
EntreLeadership, by Dave Ramsey
Good to Great, by Jim Collins
Incognito: The Secret Lives of the Brain, by David Eagleman
Aspire: Discovering your Purpose Through the Power of Words, by Kevin Hall
The Ultimate Sales Machine, by Chet Holmes
True North: Discover Your Authentic Leadership, by Bill George
Financial Peace University, by Dave Ramsey
Discovering Your Sweet Spot, by Scott M. Fay
Quiet: The Power of Introverts in a World that Can't Stop Talking, by Susan Cain
The Five Levels of Leadership, by John C. Maxwell
Who Moved My Cheese?, by Spencer Johnson
Psycho-Cybernetics, by Maxwell Maltz
As A Man Thinketh, by James Allen
The Greatest Salesman in the World, by Og Mandino
Think and Grow Rich, by Napoleon Hill
Applied Economics, by Thomas Sowell
Everyone Communicates, Few Connect, by John C. Maxwell
Getting to Yes: Negotiating Agreements, Roger Fisher, William L. Ury
Wooden: A Lifetime of Observations, by John Wooden
How Successful People Think, by John C. Maxwell
The Drucker Lectures, by Peter F. Drucker
Wealth: Is it Worth It?, by Truett S. Cathy
Put Your Dream to the Test, by John C. Maxwell

3. Paper Day Planners and Smartphone/Tablet/Computer Apps

These are the top three professional paper calendars. There are several more. The key is that you have to use it. If you don't write down the plan and then execute it, then it won't work for you. Find the one that works best for you. I have this list on my website because, as time goes on, some will be gone and new ones will appear. See http://www.roycewhite.com/planning-calendars/

Daytimer®—the original Day Planner for the serious planner. Refillable.
http://www.daytimer.com

Franklin Planner®—Just as good as a Daytimer®. Refillable.
http://franklinplanner.fcorgp.com

Dayrunner® Another great refillable calendar.
http://www.dayrunner.com/

Before I get into the App planners, I wanted to mention that I have designed an ePlanner that has a bent toward leadership and Positive Accountability. It will hopefully be ready around the end of the first quarter 2015. It will have many extra tools to help you use the accountability partnerships, as well as set goals, schedule, budget and get your life balanced. Check here often—

http:/www.roycewhite.com/eplanner

The top Apps for Apple and Android smartphones & Tablets, Mac and Windows.

iCal for IOS
Fantastical 2
Sunrise Calendar
Calendars 5
Canary
Cal

Great Blog/writup on Calendars for iPhone
http://www.idownloadblog.com/2014/03/30/best-calendar-apps-iphone/
Outlook, for windows.

4. My Definition of Success

Write your definition of success. Date it. Date any changes.

_____

_____

_____

_____

_____

_____

_____

_____

_____

_____

_____

_____

_____

_____

_____

ACCOUNTABILITY WORKSHEET

Accountability Partner 1: The person being held accountable:

_____

Phone #:_____

Text #: _____

Email address: _____

Accountability Partner 2: The person holding you accountable:

_____

Phone #:_____

Text #: _____

Email address: _____

The Topic of Accountability:

_____

_____

_____

_____

Conclusion Date: (if not ongoing)_____

When to hold accountable: (days and times)

Days:_____

Times:_____

Method of Accountability: (highly recommend Text)

❏ Phone   ❏ Text   ❏ Email   ❏ In-person

Signed_____

Signed_____

6. List of *Great* Coaches Recommended by Royce

Below are some of the finest Life/Confidence/Executive coaches you will ever come across. Not only are they highly trained and mentored *specifically* as coaches for *years*, their experience, ability, and desire to see you succeed is second to none. There are a lot more, but I simply can't possibly personally know the *individual* quality of all my 2,800+ peers on the John Maxwell Team. I *can* say, I do know their mentors and teachers and based on that alone, you have a great chance of getting one of the best coaches in the world from anyone on the John Maxwell Mentorship Team. BTW, They did not pay to be listed here—I listed them because they are very, very good. To all the JM Team members not listed, I apologize. Hopefully I will get to know you over the coming years. To all the members I *DO* know but are not listed here—I didn't get a response from you [:( ]. You can still get listed on my website. If you know I know you, and you are awesome—let me know your info and I'll get you on my website. To see a current list of names, go to roycewhite.com/coaches or click on the button marked "Coaches" at the top of the website.

When you contact them, tell them Royce's book on *Positive Accountability* sent you. They will treat you well. This is not an exhaustive list—there are a lot more on my website and the list is growing as I receive the information from those I requested and as I learn the abilities of more of the coaches. If you want to really, really, really succeed, get with one of these coaches. They are listed in the order I received their information. The information below follows this protocol—

Coach Name; *Coaching Practice Name*; Contact Phone Number; **Contact email**; *City, State location*; Hours available for coaching; *Certifications and Credentials*; URL link (Website)

Chris Warnky, *Well Done Life*; 614 896-6430; **chriswarnky@gmail.com**; *Columbus, Ohio*; M-F 7:00 am to 9:30 pm; *John Maxwell Certified Professional Coach, President of International Coaching Federation Columbus Charter Chapter, John Maxwell Team President's Advisory Council*; http://www. welldone-life.com

Joshua R. Schneider; *Prime3Coaching*; 585-727-1199; **joshua@prime3coaching.com**; *Detroit, Michigan*; 7:00am - 9:00pm EST; *John Maxwell Team Certified Coach, Level 10 Transformational Trainer*; http://www.Prime3coaching.com

Barbara Leigh; *Influential Energy*; 415-738-6380; **barbaraleigh@johnmaxwellgroup. com**; *Willemstad, Curaçao*; 7:00am - 7:00pm EST; *John Maxwell Team Certified Coach, (More at http://www.linkedin.com/pub/barbara-leigh/14/77b/918/)*; http://www.johnmaxwellgroup.com/barbaraleigh

Ria Story; *Achieve Abundant Life*; 334-332-3526; **ria.story@achieveabundantlife.com**; *Auburn, Alabama*; 7:00am - 8:00pm CST M-F; *John Maxwell Team Certified, Certified to teach group fitness: Les Mills BodyPump, BodyAttack, and RPM*; www.achieveabundantlife.com and www.johncmaxwellgroup.com/riastory

Bob Kittridge; *Kittridge Connection, Inc.*; 719-633-2097; **info@kittridgeconnection.com**; *Colorado Springs, Colorado*; Coaching Time: Open and customizable; *John Maxwell Team Certified Coach*; www.kittridgeconnection.com

Roger Nielsen; *Roger Nielsen*; 310-525-9796; **Rogernielsen73@yahoo.com**; *Los Angeles, California (Southern California)*; 6:00am - 10:00pm PST; *John Maxwell Team Certified Coach*; http:// www.rogeranielsen.com

Gloria J. Burgess; *Jazz, Inc.*; 206.954.0732; **gloria@jazz-inc.com**; *Edmonds, WA*; 8:00am – 7:00pm PST; *John Maxwell Team Certified Coach, PhD, MBA, Individual Coaching, Group Coaching*; www.gloriaburgess.com

Robert DiGiacomo; *Bermuda Bob Leadership*; 441-705-9897; **BermudaBob@me.com**; *Hamilton, Bermuda*; 7am to 11pm EST; *John Maxwell Team Certified Coach, Founding Member, President's Advisory Council, Retired Educator, Retired Officer, US Army*; BermudaBob.me

Dan Caldwell; *Caldwell & Associates, LLC*; 812-789-6240; **dancaldwell@johnmaxwellgroup.com**; *Evansville, Indiana*; 6:00 am to 6:00 pm CST; *John Maxwell Team Certified Coach, BS, MTh*; http://www.johncmaxwellgroup.com/dancaldwell/

Chandler Peterson; *Coach Chandler Peterson*; 901-860-1855; **chandlerpeterson@johnmaxwellgroup.com**; *Collierville (Memphis), Tennessee*; 8:00am - 6:00pm CST, M-F; *John Maxwell Team Certified Coach*; http://www.johnmaxwellgroup.com/chandlerpeterson

Dr. Lynn Wicker; *Center for Innovative Educational Solutions, LLC*; 850-559-9221; **lynnwicker6@gmail.com**; *Tallahassee, Florida*; :700am - 9:00pm EST; *John Maxwell Team Certified Coach, State of Florida Educational Leadership, Doctorate in Educational Leadership*; http://www.johncmaxwellgroup.com/lynnwicker/

Barry Smith; *Building What Matters, LLC*; 971-221-9495; **barry@buildingwhatmatters.com**; *Portland, Oregon*; 6:00 am - 5:00 pm PST; *John Maxwell Team Certified Coach; Author: "Leadership by Invitation"*; http://www.buildingwhatmatters.com/

Dorothy Bonvillain; *Dr. Dorothy Guy Bonvillain LLC*; 520-249-8585; **dorothybonvillain@gmail.com**; *Sierra Vista, Arizona*; 9:00am - 5:00pm PST; *John Maxwell Team certified, Kind and Caring with Integrity, High Standards and Expectations, PhD American University, Educational Administration / International Education, Leader / Coach / Author / Speaker / Trainer-Facilitator*; Books: "Loving Your Life: 7 Steps for Military Wives", "Wally Goes to School", "Traditional Handicrafts of Oman", several professional journal articles; http://www.dorothybonvillain.com

Randy Stroman; *Convergence Leadership and Relationship Center*; 855-GROW-HERE; **randy@randystroman.com**; *Dallas, Texas*; 7:00am to 5:00pm CST ; *John Maxwell Team Certified Coach, Marriage Today Certified Trainer, CFSP Level 1, CWS Level 1, Host of Pastors Exchange*; http://www.randystroman.com

Lorna Weston-Smyth; *Lorna Weston-Smyth Coaching and Training*; 416-910-4109; **Lorna@LornaWestonSmyth.com**; *Toronto, Ontario*; 7:00am - 8:00pm EST; *Certified John Maxwell Team Founding Member, Les Brown Empowerment Mentoring Program Provider, Simon Sinek Start with Why Facilitator, Member of IMPACT, International Membership of Professional Advisors, Coaches and Trainers, Member of WSA, Women's Speaker Association, Past President Business and Professional Women of Durham, Past President All Business Networkers Chapter of BNI*; http://www.lornawestonsmyth.com

Charmaine Sealey; *Charmaine Sealey*; 246 233 8142; **globaltravelsolutions@caribsurf.com**; *Barbados*; 8:30am - 4:30pm EST; *John Maxwell Team Certified Coach; Mary Gober Certified Customer Service Delivery Coach*; http://www.charmaine.sealey.com

Pete Leckemby; *Accelerate Leadership Group*; 720-552-1263; **pete@accelerateleadershipgroup.com**; *Denver, Colorado*; 8:00am - 6:00pm MST; *John Maxwell Team Certified Coach*; http://accelerateleadershipgroup.com

Terri Ayers; *WHOLE Life Coaching, Inc.*; 941-545-8697; **Terri@TerriAyers.com**; *Bradenton/Sarasota, Florida*; 6:00am - 7:00pm EST; *John Maxwell Team Certified Coach; Certified Temperament Counselor; BA in Christian Counseling, Member NCCA & SCCA, Certified AFAA PT*; http://www.TerriAyers.com

Barbara Gustavson; *Discover Next Step*; 540-429-4720; **barbara@discovernextstep.com**; *Fredericksburg, Virginia*; 9:00am - 3:00pm EST; *John Maxwell Team Certified Coach*; http://www.discovernextstep.com

Nathan Cook; *Platform-Leadership LLC*; 541-521-1142; **Nathan@platform-leadership.com**; *Portland, Oregon*; 8:00am - 5:00pm PST; *John Maxwell Team Certified Coach*; http://www.platform-leadership.com

Tom Telesco; *Telescopic Insights Group*; 702-300-5599; **Telescocoach@gmail.com**; *Las Vegas, Nevada*; 6:00am - 5:00pm PST; *John Maxwell Team Certified Coach, Life Success Consultant, Christian mentoring and coaching*; http://www.johncmaxwellgroup.com/thomastelesco, http://www.thomastelesco.com

Monica Rogers-Fletcher; *Monica Rogers-Fletcher Business Success Coach*; 868 678 9557; **mfletcher@tstt.net.tt**; *Chaguanas, Port Of Spain, Trinidad and Tobago*; 7:30a - 6:00pm EST; *John Maxwell Team Certified Coach; BSc. Agriculture Hons., Science of Success 1; Entrepreneurial Mastery; Advanced Thinking & The Psychology of Success; Science of Success 2; Business Mastery: Advanced Marketing - Leading Edge, Profit-Boosting Marketing Strategies*; http://www.johncmaxwellgroup.com/monicarogersfletcher *and* https://www.linkedin.com/profile/view?id=60764308&trk=nav_responsive_tab_profile

Mitch Tublin; *Wenkroy International LLC, America's Navigator*; 877-90-SUCCESS (877-907-8223); **info@mitchtublin.com**; *Stamford, CT*; Mutually Agreeable Hours Based Upon The Client; *ICF - PCC IPEC – MP-ELI, LMI – Master Facilitator, MBA*; http://easysmallbusinesssolutions.com

Jacqueline Burns; *JBurns Unstoppable Woman Coaching*; 310-612-5655; **info@jac-quelineburns.com**; *Dallas, TX*; 7:00pm - 9:00pm M-F; *John Maxwell Certified Speaker, Trainer, Coach*; http://jacquelineburns.com

Chris Robinson; *R3 Coaching*; 314-583-4586; **chris@r3-coaching.com**; *St. Louis, Missouri*; Hours available for coaching; *John Maxwell Team Certified Coach*; www.r3-coaching.com

Below is an additional list of some John Maxwell Team members that I know are really good coaches but I did not receive their info by publication time (they should be on my website eventually). Search for them on the John Maxwell list of coaches (see link below). And again, it's not that the other 3,00 JMT coaches are NOT really good, but that I have had presonal encounters with the people above (and below) and therefore can recommend them *directly*. I can *indirectly* recommend ALL JMT coaches.

Paula Hopwood
Sean Abbananto
Annie S. Brock
Barbara Littles
Danny Glover
Nathan Eckel
Jan Roberts
John P Griffin
Craig D Chamberlain
Dee C. Denton
Dale Wagstaff
Peggy Kimmey
Tina Black
Chris Rollins
Colin Holmes
Dave Gambril

If you don't see someone above near you, go to the John Maxwell Team Website to find someone. There are 3,000+ more world-wide listed there—

http://www.johnmaxwellgroup.com/coaches/index.php

I can't *personally* guarantee they will be great like I know the folks above to be (because I know the folks above personally), but I can say they will at least be very, very good—as good as you'll find anywhere. If you still can't find someone, email me at royce@roycewhite.com and I or one of my Community Leaders will assist you. My desire and purpose is to see you achieve and accomplish—we won't leave you hanging.

7. My Mantra "Do These Three Things and Be Content 95% of your life here on earth."

I mentioned in Chapter 4 (bottom of page 61) that I had something I wanted to tell everybody but I wasn't sure how to get people to respond and I was working on figuring that out. Nonetheless, this is the mantra I was speaking about. Here are three *Laws* that if you apply you will be content 95% of your life. These things are not the meaning of life, they are just things that will make our lives easier.

1. Budget/Schedule your time—100% of it.

Yep. Every bit of it. I do it in half hour increments, I schedule my sleep, when I go to bed, when I get up, my PT workout, meals, all work, meetings, travel—even local—free time, reading, time with kids and wife, chores. Everything. if I'm going to do it, it goes on the schedule. Studies show that if we schedule all our time, usually taking 5-15 minutes per day, we can save up to 2 hours per day. That's 730 hours per year or 5 years over a lifetime! Don't want that? Give it to me!

"The bad news is time flies. The good news is you're the pilot."
—*Michael Altshuler*

What do you save? A lot of anger from people because your late or forget. H&R Block did a study of tax filers and found that those that came in the last minute to do their taxes, paid out an additional $400 in taxes because of errors. That in itself is huge. Save a lot of money because you don't waste time. Know what's going on ALL the time so you can plan ahead and not frustrate people you double book.

Schedule your time. 100% of it. Setup your schedule a week in advance and check it the night before. Include everything. Sleep, meals, work, play, chores, free time. You will become a serious accomplisher.

Write it down. Need some tools? Daytimer, Franklin, Dayrunner. Plus a bunch on apps for your iDevice. No reason NOT to do it and everything to gain. See my Appendix 3 for planners.

2. Budget 100% of your Money. Yep. All of it.

Dave Ramsey said, "A budget is telling your money where to go instead of wondering where it went." Like scheduling your time, budgeting ALL your money ensures you have the control over it that you need. Nobody should be telling you what to spend your money on. You control every dollar. As well, like scheduling your time in the future, plan your money usage for the future. Save, invest. If you invest $2,000 per year for 10 years in mutual funds, based on the past 75 years of the market, a pretty good indicator, you should have $1.2 million waiting for you 45 years later to help you get through your final 20 years. That's a million dollars from a $20,000 investment. I don't know about you, but that's awesome to me. Can I make it $4,000 or $10,000 per year...

Sit down with your spouse or by yourself if you're not married, and create a budget for everything you spend money on. Most people think this takes away freedom wherein it really is a freedom maker. They fear that if every dollar is budgeted they won't have any money to do the things they want. That's crazy. It's still your money—budget it for the things you want AFTER you budget the things you have to budget.

I budget allowance, entertainment, entertaining—after the mortgage, utilities, doctor, clothing, car repair, house repair, vacation, savings, investments... Sometimes it's not a very big category, but it's budgeted. I know where every dollar goes. You might think that rich people don't budget. Wrong. One of the reasons they have money is precisely because they did budget. If you control every dollar, and do it wisely, you will have what you need when you want it, and be able to enjoy it all along the way.

3. Learn to communicate.

I love the George Bernard Shaw quote—"The single biggest problem in communication is the illusion that it has taken place." One of the biggest problems in life is communication... or the lack thereof. How many a forest has been set aflame by bad communication. Each of us have differing expectations—some reasonable, many, if not most, unreasonable—but mostly born out of our desire or need.

I have found that most people hint instead of communicate clearly. It is truly amazing sometimes that we can sit and talk *at* one another for 15 minutes and only hear what we have said. Communication is both a skill and an art, and the practice of it requires us to listen far more then speak and use the correct colors as we paint the picture for our hearers.

Quite frankly, I wonder sometimes if we are not merely here to share our own thoughts and nothing else, leaving the other person abandoned on the doorstep.

Read as much as you can on these three subjects and *apply* what you read. I will talk more about these things in my blog and other books because they form a major portion of our lives and a lack of ability in any of these three areas create problems.

That's it. Those three laws, if put into place and practiced diligently daily, will keep you from many a trouble, and make 95% of your life trouble free. You'll have the time and money to do what you want, and the means to interact, love, and be loved.

8. References in this Book

When there are simple definitions or general information references whose veracity is not in question, I cite Wikipedia because it is generally correct on most things, especially easy definitions (like a book reference, definition—though I usually use Dictionary.com or Mariam-webster.com for a word). For deeper and questionable items, I try to take the reference as close to the source as I can get, hopefully citing the source. In some cases there are conflicting reports/studies and hence, I will take a straddle position or get input from some of my really, really, really smart colleagues.

If you find better data on any subject, please feel compelled to send me the information. I don't care so much who is right, I just want the truth. Just don't be bombastic about it. We're all in this together. The truth forms the best outcome. It's like a guitar tuning—if you tune the A string on a guitar to 440 hz. it will (should) be in correct pitch all the way up the neck. If you tune the A to something more or less than 440 hz, it will be out of pitch on different frets on the neck. Perfect pitch, or truth, is the *physics* of true understanding.

1. *Zogby Poll Reference (page xv)*. (2014, August 6). Partners in Leadership Website Reference to Zogby Poll. Retrieved 12:38, August 6, 2014, from http://www.ozprinciple.com/others/holding-others-accountable. I have written to Zogby to get an actual copy of the study but have not received a response yet as of 2014/08/06. I will publish more info in the Errata when I receive info from Zogby. See roycewhite.com/pa-errata.

2. *When do we pay our taxes? (page xv)*. (2014, September 16). According to TurboTax, from an article by MainStreet, 41% of us file in the last four weeks before April 15, with 27% filing in the last two weeks. Retrieved 10:33, September 16, 2014, from http://www.mainstreet.com/article/when-americans-really-file-their-taxes.
Special note and because you check references (which is a good thing!) I am giving you this extra tidbit—sccording to the IRS over 70 percent of all returns filed before April 1 receive refunds, while 61 percent of returns filled late, owe money.

3. *Lord of the Flies (page xvi)*. (2014, August 3). In Wikipedia, The Free Encyclopedia. Retrieved 12:36, August 6, 2014, from http://en.wikipedia.org/w/index.php?title=Lord_of_the_Flies&oldid=619616166

4. *20% Self-Starters (page xvi)*. I read many articles and books on self-starters. Although there doesn't appear to be any specific studies on who is and isn't a self starter, I gleaned input that indicated that only about 15-24% of us are true self starters. As well, I asked a brilliant friend, business consultant and coach, whose

specialty is on transitioning business ownership between generations (i.e. father to son) what he thought the number to be. He believes the number of self-starters to be more around the number of businesses that succeed in the long run—about 12%. I agreed. As well, the statistics on procrastination lends some credibility to this number. 85-95% of people say they procrastinate from time to time. 26% say they are chronic procrastinators—and that number is on the rise (*The Nature of Procrastination: A Meta-Analytic and Theoretical Review of Quintessential Self-Regulatory Failure*, by Piers Steel, University of Calgary, 2007—http://studiemetro. au.dk/fileadmin/www.studiemetro.au.dk/Procrastination_2.pdf). Finally, looking at the Pareto Principle (Pareto principle. (2014, October 17). In Wikipedia, The Free Encyclopedia. Retrieved 18:12, October 30, 2014, from http://en.wikipedia.org/w/index.php?title=Pareto_principle&oldid=629944446), I made a presumption that 20% of us are not self starters. Taking all those factors into account, I did some interpolation, and ended with 20%. Though I accept any number from 12-24%. The point is that it's still, at best, only a quarter of us that truly self-finish. 75% of us give up somewhere in the race. Even if the number were 50%, there is a large percentage of us that don't fully get where we want to go. Wherein I believe this book contains a lot of good information for everyone, it is those that have trouble getting started that I want to help the most.

5. *Don White (page xvii, 7, 12, 44)*. Dad, engineer extrodinaire, math modeler, author of some 15+ books on engineering... (Throughout my life...). Retrieved 10:11, August 6, 2014 from my memory...

6. *81% have a book in them (page xvii)*. "According to a recent survey, 81 percent of Americans feel they have a book in them—and that they should write it." (2002, September 2). In The New York Times. Retrieved 10:17, August 6, 2014, from http://www.nytimes.com/2002/09/28/opinion/28EPST.html?ex=1149220800&en=d9acea65786f91da&ei=5070

7. *What percent start businesses (page xvii)*. (May 27, 2013). In Forbes. Retrieved 23:07, August 6, 2014, from http://www.forbes.com/sites/elainepofeldt/2013/05/27/u-s-entrepreneurship-hits-record-high/

8. *Eat That Frog (page xviii)*. Brian Tracy's website—http://www.briantracy.com/catalog/eat-that-frog-2nd-edition—Retrieved 18:44, August 6, 2014. Purchase from Amazon- http://www.amazon.com/Eat-That-Frog-Great-Procrastinating/dp/1576754227/ref=sr_1_1?ie=UTF8&qid=1407350487&sr=8-1&keywords=brian+tracy+eat+that+frog

9. *Order of Magnitude (page xix)*. Typically means 10 times. Order of magnitude. (2014, July 5). In Wikipedia, The Free Encyclopedia. Retrieved 18:32, August 6, 2014, from http://en.wikipedia.org/w/index.php?title=Order_of_magnitude&oldid=615664030

10. *The story of Naaman (page 3)*. (Antiquity 560-538 B.C.) In the Hebrew/Christian Bible. Retrieved 18:34, August 6, 2014, from The new American Standard Bible, 2 Kings 5.

11. *Snake oil (page 5)*. An expression that originally referred to fraudulent health products or unproven medicine but has come to refer to any product with questionable or unverifiable quality or benefit. By extension, a snake oil salesman is someone who knowingly sells fraudulent goods or who is himself or herself a fraud, quack, charlatan, and the like. Snake oil. (2014, July 19). In Wikipedia, The Free Encyclopedia. Retrieved 13:23, July 21, 2014, from http://en.wikipedia.org/w/index.php?title=Snake_oil&oldid=617640849

12. *The 15 Invaluable Laws of Growth: Live Them and Reach Your Potential (page xvi, 5)*. Maxwell, John C. (2012-10-02). Center Street. Kindle Edition. Retrieved 19:00, August 6, 2014. Purchase from Amazon—http://www.amazon.com/The-Invaluable-Laws-Growth-Potential/dp/1599953668/ref=sr_1_1?ie=UTF8&qid=1407351736&sr=8-1&keywords=the+15+invaluable+laws+of+growth

13. *Only about 58% of people read after college (page 8)*. Also, statistic about *Total percentage of U.S. families who did not buy a book this year (page 8)*. (July 14, 2014). Statistics Brain. Retrieved 19:27, August 6, 2014 from http://www.statisticbrain.com/reading-statistics

14. *92% Jenny Craig Study (page 12)*. (May 10, 2011). *"I suspect that the one-on-one coaching sessions are particularly instrumental in helping people stick to their weight loss while in the program," Scirica said. "Presumably, however, people do not stay in the program indefinitely and, although the Jenny Craig program reportedly teaches them the skills needed to maintain their weight loss after leaving, one cannot say from this study whether those efforts actually work."* (Royce Note: Don't know what the final outcome will be on keeping off the weight, but I believe the main reason people stuck with it was because they had a Positive Accountability partner in their coach. There is a bit of controversy surrounding the findings, but for the point we are making, the data is intact. Retrieved 20:06, August 6, 2014 from ABC News http://abcnews.go.com/US/kentucky-floating-restaurant-sinks-river/story?id=24868010

15. *Christian Simpson (page 13)*. The main mentor and teacher for the John Maxwell Team for coaching. Christian is a Master Coach and entrepreneurial business trainer. He teaches *and* mentors the *Art, Science, and Practice of Coaching* and has trained thousands of individuals over the past 14 years. His humble demeanor and exceptional coaching ability have helped him to replicate his ability to those on the John Maxwell team. Much of what I know regarding coaching comes from his diligent efforts to pass on his vast coaching knowledge and experience. I owe him a great gratitude of thanks. Thank you Christian!

16. *21 Days to build a habit Myth (page 14)*. (April 15, 2013). Forbes. Retrieved 14:28, September 16, 2014 from http://www.forbes.com/sites/jasonselk/2013/04/15/habit-formation-the-21-day-myth/

17. *Lemmings Myth* (page 14). http://www.snopes.com/disney/films/lemmings.asp

18. *Three Phases of Habit Formation (page 14)*. (April 15, 2013). Developed by Tom Bartow and Dr. Jason Selk. Forbes. Retrieved 14:28, September 16, 2014 from http://www.forbes.com/sites/jasonselk/2013/04/15/habit-formation-the-21-day-myth/

19. *The Ultimate Sales Machine (page 20)*. Chet Holms Website—http://www.chetholmes.com/the-ultimate-sales-machine.php —Retrieved 18:54, August 6, 2014. Purchase from Amazon—http://www.amazon.com/dp/1591842158/?tag=googhydr-20&hvadid=35271748681&hvpos=1t1&hvexid=&hvnetw=g&hvrand=7128961010239780780&hvpone=10.20&hvptwo=32&hvqmt=b&hvdev=c&ref=pd_sl_8dafixpj8_b

20. *Howard Hill (page 31)*. (2014, September 7). In Wikipedia, The Free Encyclopedia. Retrieved 18:37, September 16, 2014, from http://en.wikipedia.org/w/index.php?title=Howard_Hill&oldid=624563739

21. *People give up looking for a career (page 35)*. Not 100% sure because I cannot find any reference online, but I recall from my early days reading and listening to Zig Ziglar that he used this quote to show that we give up pursuing our true dream when we get a job that meets our general needs. It's good to be working, but continue to pursue your passion, your calling.

22. *48 Days to the Work You Love (page 36)*. Miller, Dan C. (2010). B&H Publishing Group. Kindle Edition. Retrieved 09:04, August 7, 2014. Purchase from Amazon—http://www.amazon.com/Days-Work-You-Love-Preparing/dp/1433669331/ref=sr_1_1?ie=UTF8&qid=1407416487&sr=8-1&keywords=48+days+to+the+work+you+love

23. *Scott Fay, What do you really, really, really want (page 37)*. Scott is The Vice President of the John Maxwell Team and one of the teams mentors. His book, *Discover Your Sweet Spot: The 7 Steps to Create a Life of Success and Significance*, is a good read and helps point you toward success. You can purchase from Amazon—http://www.amazon.com/Discover-Your-Sweet-Spot-Significance-ebook/dp/B00F2KZ95O/ref=sr_1_1?ie=UTF8&qid=1410893703&sr=8-1&keywords=scott+fay

24. *Rate of Business Closures (page 43).* SBA statistics on small business. Retrieved 15:35, September 16, 2014. http://www.sba.gov/sites/default/files/FAQ_March_2014_0.pdf

25. *Throwing in the Towel (page 44).* http://www.knowyourphrase.com/phrase-meanings/Throw-In-the-Towel.html
"This phrase is believed to come from boxing, where the coach, or perhaps a teammate, would literally throw a towel into the ring in ordr to signal that his fighter has been defeated; it was basically a way to surrender. This term has been around since the very start of the 1900s."

26. *Zeigarnik Effect Study (page 45). 2) Your brain procrastinates on big projects by visualizing the worst parts.* Retrieved 15:42, September 16, 2014. http://blog.buffer-app.com/how-our-brains-stop-us-achieving-our-goals-and-how-to-fight-back

27. *Our brain doesn't like Information gaps (page 50).* (5/15/2012). Retrieved 13:23, September 17, 2014 from http://www.forbes.com/sites/work-in-progress/2012/05/15/10-brainteasers-to-test-your-mental-sharpness/

28. *Nadia Comenica (page 58).* (2014, June 23). In Wikipedia, The Free Encyclopedia. Retrieved 13:13, July 4, 2014, from http://en.wikipedia.org/w/index.php?title=Nadia_Com%C4%83neci&oldid=614147711

29. *Otitis Interna (page 58).* (2014, March 25). In Wikipedia, The Free Encyclopedia. Retrieved 13:11, July 4, 2014, from http://en.wikipedia.org/w/index.php?title=Otitis_interna&oldid=601149448

30. *Aspire—Discovering Your Purpose Through the Power of Words (page 59).* Hall, Kevin. (2009, 2010) HarperCollins e-books Kindle Edition. Purchase from Amazon http://www.amazon.com/Aspire-Discovering-Purpose-Through-Power-ebook/dp/B003100URE/ref=sr_1_1?s=books&ie=UTF8&qid=1410897225&sr=1-1&keywords=aspire+discovering+your+purpose+through+the+power+of+words

31. *Mint.com (page 61).* Mint is a great app for tracking your money from Intuit—the makers of Quicken, TurboTax, and QuickBooks—account software experts.. It ties into all your accounts so you have all the most current info, allows budgeting so you can see where your spending is. It's a great tool for keeping an eye on where your money and investments go. See more at http://www.mint.com

32. *Eat drink and be merry (page 61).* (Antiquity before ~931 B.C.) In the Hebrew/Christian Bible. Retrieved 16:01, September 16, 2014, from The new American Standard Bible, Ecclesiastes 8:15—https://www.biblegateway.com/passage/?search=Ecclesiastes+8:15&version=NASB

33. *21 Irrefutable Laws of Leadership: Follow Them and People Will Follow You (page 65)*. Maxwell, John C. (2007). Thomas Nelson. Kindle Edition. Retrieved 08:58, August 7, 2014. Purchase from Amazon—http://www.amazon.com/The-Irrefutable-Laws-Leadership-Anniversary/dp/0785288376/ref=sr_1_1?ie=UTF8&qid=1407416 373&sr=8-1&keywords=21+irrefutable+laws+of+leadership .

34. *What happens when we get angry? (page 66)*. Science Daily Study Plataforma SINC, 1 June 2010. Retrieved 14:12, September 16, 2014 from http://www.science-daily.com/releases/2010/05/100531082603.htm>

35. *"Don't Drive Angry!" (page 67*. Bill Murry to the groundhog in the movie *Groundhog Day*. Retrieved 14:31, September 18, 2014 from https://www.youtube.com/watch?v=uBpw1sdFu2w&feature=kp

36. *Common Sense is not Common Practice (page 69*. I've seen this quote credited to Stephen Covey, Will Rogers and Voltaire, who said, "Common sense is not so common."

37. *Chris Warnky (page 73)*. John Maxwell Team member. Excellent Life/Executive Coach, Columbus, Ohio. 614 896-6430. Call him. Today. You'll be glad you did.

38. *Lion of Androcles (page 74)*. Asops Fables. Androcles. (2014, August 11). In Wikipedia, The Free Encyclopedia. Retrieved 18:40, September 18, 2014, from http://en.wikipedia.org/w/index.php?title=Androcles&oldid=620732160

39. *Financial Peace University (page 96)*. Great tool for getting on budget and building wealth! Purchase from Uncle Dave at http://www.daveramsey.com/store/finan-cial-peace-university/financial-peace-university-membership-all-new/prod614.html?ectid=gaw.fpu-general1&gclid=CjwKEAjwv9-gBRD5ofn2jd2N0UUS-JACcdilsbX9_KnikNvoBI49kgrO87V4ILmgiqu4XLH4kQwH6TxoCwxXw_wcB

40. *Number of American Combat Deaths (page 98)*. United States military casualties of war. (2014, October 13). In Wikipedia, The Free Encyclopedia. Retrieved 20:01, October 15, 2014, from http://en.wikipedia.org/w/index.php?title=United_States_military_casualties_of_war&oldid=629371690 The quality and number of references cited in the wiki listing is quite significant and acceptable for my reference purpose.

41. *Yada, Yada, Yada (page 100)*. Means boring or of little information value. Sometimes used instead of etc., etc., etc. More of the same. Retrieved definition 16:35, September 16, 2014 from http://www.merriam-webster.com/dictionary/yada%20yada

42. *Porn Monitoring Software (page 106).* Software used to monitor your computers and devices and let you know what's being seen. http://www.covenanteyes.com/family/?ibp-adgroup=adwords&ibp-keyword=covenant%20eyes&ibp-matchtype=e&ibp-custom=1t1&gclid=CjwKEAjwv9-gBRD5ofn2jd2N0UUS-JACcdilsMmb0okwXkfb7pMDP78fq_2mIEFnYKIBoA3z5E9Cf8hoCvE_w_wcB

43. *Do it Fifty Times (page 108).* Author and motivational speaker W. Clement Stone encouraged his audience, "Before you get out of bed every morning, say 'do it now' fifty times. At the end of the day before you go to sleep, the last thing you should do is say 'do it now' fifty times." Maxwell, John C. (2012-10-02). The 15 Invaluable Laws of Growth: Live Them and Reach Your Potential (p. 11). Center Street. Kindle Edition.

44. *15 Minutes of daily planning can save two hours a day (page 111).* "The good news is that every minute spent in planning saves as many as ten minutes in execution. It takes only about 10 to 12 minutes for you to plan out your day, but this small investment of time will save you up to two hours (100 to 120 minutes) in wasted time and diffused effort throughout the day." Tracy, Brian (2007-01-01). *Eat That Frog!: 21 Great Ways to Stop Procrastinating and Get More Done in Less Time* (Kindle Locations 270-272). Berrett-Koehler Publishers. Kindle Edition.

45. *Planner Apps (page 111).* See the Appendix page 147 for paper and app oriented daily calendars.

46. *We are all creative (page 117).* Leo Widrich article *Why We Have Our Best Ideas in the Shower: The Science of Creativity.* 02/28/2013. Retrieved 9/16/2014, from http://blog.bufferapp.com/why-we-have-our-best-ideas-in-the-shower-the-science-of-creativity

47. *How fast do dreams dissipate? (page 117.* DreamScience. Retrieved 19:45, September 16, 2014 from http://www.dreamscience.org/idx_faq.htm

48. *Skin in the Game (page 118).* Skin in the game (phrase). (2014, May 3). In Wikipedia, The Free Encyclopedia. Retrieved 19:44, July 16, 2014, from http://en.wikipedia.org/w/index.php?title=Skin_in_the_game_(phrase)&oldid=606944951

9. Errata

An Errata is usually a sheet of paper added to a printed book immediately after the book is printed, with corrections that happened after the book went to press. In today's world of POD—Print on Demand, you can usually make changes right up to the last minute. However, things will still get caught after it is put to bed. I am going to use this for corrections, new discoveries, different thoughts and other related things, new links, similar concepts, debunked theories, new brain studies, great chicken recipes... well... See

http://www.roycewhite.com/pa-errata/

for up to the moment corrections, changes, and additions to the book.

Thank you!

Current Keynote, Workshops, and Training Courses
(All these can be 45 minute Keynote, 90 minute workshop, or full day Seminar)

Positive Accountability – The First Step to Success.
80% of us are not self-starters or self-finishers. Getting to our definition of success eludes us more than we care to admit. It doesn't have to. We can take life by storm and make it work for us. Learn the methodology of Positive Accountability and be on the other side of accomplishment. In this seminar, each of us will discover our true passion, build our own definition of success, work towards life balance, gain the proper attitude to succeed, apply personal leadership principles, learn how to stay on target, and then literally put a system into place that will walk us through to success.

Growing and Prospering Your Small Business.
This is for anyone who has a small business or who is thinking about starting one. Sometimes we start a business with no more than an idea and a lot of coffee. Unfortunately, we can miss a lot of important steps and fail quickly – or come dangerously close to failing and end up with lots of debt. As entrepreneurs, the statistics don't help us much – we still dive in know that we have at best a 50:50 chance of survival. I've started seven businesses in my life, most prospered but some failed. I've failed forward and put together this seminar on how to run a profitable business. From finances, to production, to marketing and a whole lot more in-between. A lot of it is having the proper attitude and doing the right thing at the right time, losing your self-limiting fears while embracing the proper fears. Come learn how to take your business from where it is to where you want it to be.

Marketing Your Small Business 101.
Marketing is a lot more than advertising. It's knowing what product mix to sell. How best to sell it. Pricing. Competition. Statistical analysis. Plus, there are a gazillion ways to advertise out there. Email. On-Line. Adwords. Snail mail. Direct mail. This seminar will show you how to determine what works in your industry/business. We will tackle the methodology behind any ad campaign – the real principles that matter. This seminar will not tell you what the best places are to advertise because that is different for each company/industry/product. Anybody that tells you otherwise is trying to sell you something. BUT I will show you how to figure it out, test it inexpensively, and then learn to roll-out the advertising to maximize your sales and profitability. It's not rocket science. But it is logical and anybody can do it. You just have to know what questions to ask.

Life Intentional.
Do you have a personal plan for your life? If not, why not? If you are not intentional about your life, if you're not really, really, really serious about achieving your goals, if you don't have a proven system and process – you won't get there. If you're ready when opportunity comes, and you apply your knowledge, you can succeed. We're going to look at what it takes to live life intentionally, immediately, and specifically. We're going to study the methodology and procedures necessary and help you put them in place to get where you really want to go. We're also going to show you how to finish what you begin so you will get to accomplishment. If you're not deciding how to live your life, then somebody else is. It's time to stop being a victim, take control of your life, and live it to the fullest.

Get a Free Copy of My eBook—Profitable Marketing Concepts
(www.roycewhite.com)

Google. Facebook. Adwords. Email. Direct Mail. Snail Mail. Print media. Radio. TV. You-tube. There are a gazillion ways for you to spend your cash on unproven marketing methods. Unproven?? Really? Yep. All of them are unproven. At least unproven by you. Okay. Maybe you've been advertising and doing just fine thank you – or at least making a profit.

Great. So if it's not proven, why is Google so huge? Because there are a lot of people that don't know whether their advertising dollars are really profitable. We make quick decisions and spend the money and get a questionable return – or worse – an unknown return. I've spent tens of millions of dollars on marketing campaigns and have developed a tactical strategy that helps increase your marketing return – no matter where you are in your current plan you can increase your ROI. A simple five step methodology that if applied consistently will have a major impact on the quality of your advertising campaigns.

By my estimate over the past 35 years, only about 2% of the business population has a real grasp on marketing concepts. I don't say this to impress you, but to impress upon you that it's not uncommon to not be versed in marketing. Most of us spend our time on the production of our products – as Michael Gerber coined, we work *in* our business instead of *on* our business. My product just happened to be marketing.

So before you spend your first marketing dollar – or before you spend any more of your hard earned cash – you need to embrace some of the basic concepts of marketing advertising. This is a short eBook that covers the five basic marketing principles of advertising so no matter what method you choose, you can ensure you don't waste money on bad decisions. You can only get these principles by signing up to get my daily blog. My desire is to invest in you because you have invested your time in me by reading my blog. I don't take that lightly. This way you never miss the daily walk toward success. It's a win-win. No-brainer. Sign up here or on any page in the upper right corner.

In all candor, to the extent you follow these marketing five laws, you will be more successful with your advertising and sales campaigns. These are the principles of understanding in adver-tising – the physics of it all. Plus, I will expand and add to these in the Marketing portion of my blog so this will give you a great basis to launch from. Feel free to ask questions about anything you may not understand. Either I or one of my Community Leaders will answer to clarify.

These concepts are simple – it isn't rocket science. But like so many other pieces of knowl-edge, we don't apply it – it just sits there taking up space. Apply each of these – make it a checkoff-list for each campaign and make your advertising soar. Even if you only apply it a little.

Why is this so valuable? Every dollar I have spent on a campaign is an investment in educa-tion because I learned from that dollar. So in reality, you're getting tens of millions of dollars of experience.

Sign up today to receive my blogs by email and start increasing the profitability of your mar-keting. (go to roycewhite.com)

You cannot change the past... BUT, you can change now to affect the future, and, by doing that, you can change the outcome of your entire life.

Royce White

www.ingramcontent.com/pod-product-compliance
Lightning Source LLC
Chambersburg PA
CBHW071434090426
42737CB00011B/1658